f-words
mom let us say:
food, family & friends

f-words mom let us say: food, family & friends
everyday recipes that will make you feel loved

Published by Sharon Caldwell Peddie, LLC.
www.sharoncaldwellpeddie.com

ISBN: 979-8-9866323-1-5
First Edition 2022, United States

This book does not replace the advice of your medical professional.
Consult your physician for any changes to your diet or health plan.

Our recipes have been tried and used successfully by us.
Products used for cooking, ingredient choices,
substitutions, etc., may affect recipe outcomes.

Editor, Deri Reed | *Book Cover and Interior Design,* Julie Karen Hodgins
Copy Editor, Indexer, Proofreader, Heather Pendley | *Photo Editor,* Dorothy Durling
Front Cover Image, Suzanne Young Photography | *Back Cover Image,* Taylor Yob

f-words

mom let us say:
food, family & friends

everyday recipes that will make you feel loved

Sharon Caldwell Peddie

Kelsey Peddie

Kendall Peddie

Cameron Peddie

table of contents

introduction

Welcome to our cookbook and our family; we're so excited you're here! I coauthored this cookbook with my three girls, Kelsey, Kendall, and Cami.

Our cookbook was created during the covid-19 pandemic. I'll try to set the stage for you quickly. Kelsey and Kendall each have their own place not too far from our family home. After college, they were excited to be out on their own with careers and homes. Cami, our youngest and still in college, had just arrived home for spring break. And then—BAM!—the global pandemic. As we all remember too well, we were asked to "shelter in place" to prevent the spread. Not knowing how long that would be or how isolated everyone would feel, our family decided to stick close and shelter under one roof to navigate it together.

So, Kelsey and Kendall came home as well. We quickly turned every inch of our home into offices for my husband, a sportswear exec; Kelsey, a business attorney; Kendall, a registered dietitian; Cami, a strategic communications and fine arts student; and me, an author. With everyone trying to work and not get in each other's way, it was challenging, to say the least. But also pretty funny and fun. At the end of each day, we found ourselves gathering in the kitchen to help each other process covid-19 times. Cooking and sitting around the table together was the highlight of our quarantine. The kitchen became the place where we shared our daily struggles and victories, just like we did when the girls were growing up. On weeknights, we cooked favorite family recipes for comfort, and on the weekends, we challenged ourselves by trying to recreate dishes we were missing from our favorite restaurants. Cooking together felt very therapeutic.

It was on one of our exciting, pandemic Saturday nights that we decided to make gnocchi, after being "bored in the house and in the house bored." (If you watched lots of TikTok like us, you get the reference.) Sure, we hadn't made gnocchi before, but we're always a strong team in the kitchen and we certainly had the time, so why not? With some fun music, a little wine, and combining and altering a few well-researched recipes, gnocchi night was a fun and delicious success! It was a special night that helped remind us of how resilient we are and capable of creating our own fun and light in dark times. More importantly, that was the night the idea for our cookbook was born. But really, after our years and fun in the kitchen together, we feel like the cookbook chose us.

As a mom of three girls, it's been my passion and mission to raise confident women with a strong sense of self. There are many roads to help build that, and we've traveled many of them—from academics, sports, arts, community service, and more. But one of my biggest surprises was seeing how learning to cook proved to be such a powerful road to developing my girls' self-love and confidence. (I think I should also include myself in that as well.) Cooking has been a more-fun and less-pressure-packed way to build confidence than some of those other roads. It was often a nice break from a busy and competitive world, and it still is! We're excited to share that experience with you and hope it inspires women and men, girls and boys of all ages to get into the kitchen to grow. None of us are too young or too old to grow, and cooking truly helps us and our lives grow more meaningfully beautiful!

I think my love of cooking stems from my dad's side of the family. Southerners are all about the food, and all of my dad's family were enthusiastic cooks from Mississippi. Whether someone's coming to dinner or the sky just happens to be blue that day, Southerners are ready to whip up something delicious. I learned that cooking for family and friends is one of the purest ways to show our love. That Southern way of sharing love through cooking is something I treasured being a part of, and I knew I wanted to carry that philosophy forward as I raised my own family.

The girls grew up in the kitchen with me. We've always loved creating family meals together, and we love a kitchen or backyard full of friends! Hosting dance team celebrations, soccer and volleyball team sleepovers, and backyard dinner parties was a way of life. Each of my girls had at least one friend that immediately went to the pantry when they came over because they knew we probably had a delicious homemade snack in there. Whatever the occasion, we've enthusiastically made something from our hearts. Over the years, we've developed traditions around food that mean the world to us. They have become the fabric of our lives—and our friends' lives too. When the kids were young, we did backyard shrimp boils to raise money for their schools. We've hosted mother/daughter Christmas cookie exchanges with over 100 friends every year for 22 years. Each summer, we have a giant paella party in our backyard. Each time we've created together, we've grown. We've grown as cooks. We've grown as people. We've grown our bonds within our family and in our community.

Being together, cooking, creating, and writing our cookbook has been our pandemic silver lining. Putting our recipes, experiences, values, philosophies, and memories in writing has felt so powerful. It feels like a positive, productive punch at covid-19 and kind of a metaphoric f*** *you.* Our cookbook is a celebration of positivity, resiliency, and creating a beautiful life no matter what—and we want to share that spirit with you. We understand more than ever that food, family, and friends (faith, of course, too) are the most beautiful, meaningful, and nourishing F words. They are the words that life is all about.

We are not professional chefs and don't pretend to be. But, we are experienced, creative home cooks who put love into everything we cook! We believe you'll feel the love in our recipes, and in turn, you will feel loved when you make them yourself. We truly believe they are recipes you'll want to make over and over again. We are so grateful you chose our cookbook and that now we're all a part of each other's lives. Open our door, flip the pages, and come on in. We're waiting for you!

love, sharon, kelsey, kendall, and cami

peddie kitchen commandments

family philosophies from our kitchen

view cooking as an important gift to ourselves.

We often hear people say that they don't want to go through the trouble of cooking if it's just for them alone. Food is our lifeline in so many ways, and if we don't nurture and fuel *ourselves* through food, who will? How will we care for our family and friends if we don't nurture and fuel ourselves first? Each time we plan, shop, and create a meal, we are communicating to ourselves that we are worthy! Cooking for ourselves is a daily self-care affirmation that grows our self-love, self-confidence, and self-esteem. Cooking for ourselves also allows us to be in the driver's seat of our own health because we know what's going into our bodies. The more we cook for ourselves, the more positive we can make our relationship with food. The more positive a relationship we have with food, the more beautiful example we set for those we love.

think of cooking as a beautiful gift we give others.

Cooking for others is an act of love. As humans, we need food, love, and connection to survive. Each time we cook for someone, we are nourishing them in many ways. We are building their fuel, inner joy, and feelings of connection. We love to share our love through cooking for our family and friends. It has such important benefits for everyone's mind, body, and soul. Cooking for others is a beautiful gift.

use teamwork to make the dream work.

Making the dream work has always been a guiding philosophy in our family. While we don't view cooking as a chore, we don't deny that there is work involved. Our family ethos is that everyone needs to work together for each member and the whole team to thrive. We all cook for each other. At times, we wait on each other. We definitely clean up after each other. We take turns so everyone can feel valued and nurtured.

make and keep traditions with family and friends.

When you create traditions around food, family, and friends, you create beautiful lasting bonds! Create traditions with the people you love and be committed to keeping them.

cherish sunday night family dinners.

If you are blessed to have family in your home or close by, choose a night to prioritize each other and come together for a meal. Life can get so busy, and before you know it, long periods can go by without loved ones sitting at the same table. Our family time is Sunday dinner. It's usually one of the slower nights of the week for all of us and has always been a good way to start a new week feeling centered and part of a strong team.

be present.

We believe that whether you're cooking alone or with others, being present is a gift. Being a good cook requires being very present, but being present in the kitchen isn't *just* about being a good cook. It's about enjoying the soulful, nurturing, creative experience that's waiting for you there. Don't steal that from yourself or the people you're cooking with and for. Cooking can be very therapeutic and encourages bonding. Slow down when you can. Breathe deeply. Feed your mind and soul while preparing food to feed your body. Try to leave the world and worries out of the kitchen. Just be there for yourself and for whoever you're cooking with. Being present is a valuable present.

be bold. be brave in the kitchen.

Just like anything in life, when we push ourselves to try new experiences, we develop our confidence and self-esteem. And the more you push yourself as a cook, the more successful you become. Dive into cookbooks and keep trying new recipes that sound delicious. Try recipes that seem hard. Embrace mistakes and try again. Perfect your favorite foods. Try new cooking techniques and tools to create foods you never thought you could. The more successful you are, the more confident you become, and that's a gift you get to take into the world with you!

try new foods often.

Try something new! Every food you eat has its own unique nutritional and flavor profile. Traveling, eating at different restaurants, and going to friends' houses for dinner all inspire us to expand our flavor comfort zone and add to our nutritional profile. So buy pasta made with different plants, experiment with different kinds of milk, incorporate seasonal produce into your meals, add different nuts and seeds to your snacks, and vary your protein choices.

remember that there's no such thing as perfect.

Perfection doesn't exist anywhere and it's not supposed to! There is no such thing as a perfect person or a perfect chef. Our philosophy for cooking is to create nutritious, favorite meals that nurture and nourish ourselves and others. Sometimes, what we create turns out to be a beautiful, cookbook- or Pinterest-worthy dish and sometimes, well, it just doesn't. Who cares if it's not perfect? Each time we make something from our hands and heart, we are growing in our skills, confidence, self-love, and self-esteem. Don't be afraid to cook anything. Try it—amaze yourself!

bring music into the kitchen.

When you combine food and music, you are setting yourself up to feel and thrive, because both are nourishment for the mind, body, and soul. Listening to music while we cook is way more of a fun vibe; it also inspires creativity and feelings and that's when magic happens! We often like to match our music to the types of food we're cooking. Spotify playlists are awesome!

invest in good oils and different spices. Grow herbs.

Good olive oil, a variety of spices, and fresh herbs will lead you to healthier cooking and eating and are better ways to build flavor profiles than adding excessive salt. If you can look at these as cooking essentials, your food will taste better and will make for more flavorful, nutritious results.

shop and cook for the season.

You don't have to cook expensive foods to make good food, but really good, fresh ingredients will always taste expensive! For the freshest ingredients at the best prices, shop and cook for the season. Try recipes that include foods grown in that season, because that's what will be freshest at your store. We love a farmers' market; they always steer menu planning in the right direction.

think about ways you can repurpose ingredients in other dishes.

It's such a waste to buy a bunch of ingredients and use them just one time. Before buying ingredients for just one recipe, think of other recipes you can use them in throughout the week. Reducing food waste is better for the environment and our wallets.

start with a clean kitchen, wash your hands, and keep washing all the way through.

Cooking is much more enjoyable when you start with a clean, tidy kitchen. Cooking is a messy job, so don't overwhelm yourself by starting behind the eight ball. Your head will feel much more organized which makes cooking safer, low to no stress, and fun!

read a new recipe three times: the first to shop, the second to prep, and the third to cook.

Increase confidence and success with a new recipe by committing to reading it in its entirety three times. Before shopping, read the recipe, check your supplies, and write a list of ingredients you need. Read the recipe again while gathering the ingredients to remind yourself how they need to be prepped. Then, boost your confidence by reading it one more time before turning on the oven or stove.

mise en place!

Okay, we are a little silly, but this is one of our favorite things to say in the kitchen. *Mise en place* is a French culinary term meaning "put in place" or "everything in its place." Not only is it a fun phrase, but it's also one of the most helpful ways to ensure the success of your dish. If equipment is ready and all of the ingredients are prepped before cooking, it eliminates stress and makes cooking more fun. It's worth a few extra dirty dishes. A set of clear bowls in various sizes sell for about $25 to $40 and make for the best *mise en place* tools. Place your prepped ingredients (chopped, sliced, or grated and measured) into the bowls, arrange them all on a rimmed baking sheet, and you are automatically imbued with magical cheffy powers.

cook with all five senses.

The best key to success in the kitchen is to cook with all five senses. Seeing, touching, smelling, tasting, and listening is like getting help from five different chefs. **Look** to see that the pot isn't boiling over and when the meat is lifting from the pan and is ready to flip. **Smell** the garlic to be sure it's not getting ready to burn. Let your nose alert you that the cookies are close to done. **Listen** for the snaps, crackles, and pops of hot oil to signal that the heat needs to be adjusted. **Touch** the baking bread to see if it springs back, and pierce a boiling potato with a fork to check if it's done. **Taste** a dish at various stages so you know what is needed to enhance its flavor. It's not enough to just follow a recipe; we need all our senses to increase the odds of creating a successful dish.

practice and perfect your knife skills.

Knife skills are vital to efficient cooking, reduce prep time, and increase safety. Treat yourself to at least one good chef's knife and a good paring knife. Watch a few tutorials for efficient, safe techniques, and then practice. Find what feels natural but keep peeling, chopping, slicing, and dicing. Equally important is keeping your knives sharp. Accidents seem to happen more with dull knives than sharp ones.

refrain from negative food talk, food shaming, and obsessing over calories.

Be mindful and refrain from unhealthy conversations about calories, giving food moral value by labeling it "good" or "bad," and judging people for what they do or do not eat. We believe in whole-body health. We believe food is nourishment for the mind, body, and soul. We believe that all foods can be enjoyed without a side of guilt or shame. If you value nourishing your body, mind, and soul, you will intuitively seek a daily variety of plants, proteins, carbs, and yes, sweets and treats too!

add, don't subtract.

Instead of focusing on restricting or cutting out certain foods or food groups, we would rather focus on what we can add to our life and eating patterns. We think it's an easier approach to add more color, more plants, more variety, and/or more balance to promote health.

practice mindful eating as an act of self-love.

When it comes to the actual cooking and eating, we take the time to breathe, relax, and make loving choices for our mind, body, and soul. Mindfulness begins as we make the decision of what to eat and as we prepare the meal, then continues as we relax, breathe, and truly savor every bite of the fruits of our labor. And without stressing, we can also be a bit mindful about how much to eat—when to keep going, and when to stop. But none of us are perfect, so be kind to yourself: Maybe we ate past fullness or didn't eat the right thing we needed at the time. So what? Being mindful of the way you talk to yourself helps you get it better the next time.

don't salt at every stage.

We are not anti-salt. We know sodium is necessary for our bodies and that it can add incredible flavor. We do try to use less salt, though, since an excess can be detrimental to our health over time. You will see "kosher salt and freshly ground black pepper to taste" in most of our recipes. This is because every palate is different, so we leave it up to you how much salt to use. We recommend tasting often and trying to add only what's needed to bring out the best flavors and textures.

You'll see that most of our recipes call for unsalted butter. You can use salted if that's what you have on hand or what your taste buds are used to and it will not ruin the recipe. However, you might want to cut back on any additional salt in the recipe.

use your beautiful dishes and create a beautiful table for a beautiful life!

We are not wait-for-a-special-occasion-to-set-a-pretty-table kind of people. Life is made up of more normal days than special occasions, so we like to make a normal day feel special. You cared to cook something beautiful, so why not celebrate by using pretty plates, lovely shaped glasses, and colorful cloth napkins? In a technology-intensive world, we are sensory deprived. When we create simple beauty around us, it feels good to our souls. Grow your life more sensorily beautiful; you deserve it!

share your food. share your recipes. share your love.

Sharon's grandmother used to say, "Don't trust anyone who won't share their recipe." That's pretty funny, but she was right. Recipes are like love and they're meant to be shared. We love and embrace that philosophy and we wrote a cookbook to prove it!

share your recipes. share your food. share your love.

some of our favorite kitchen items

Sometimes, we don't know what's missing in the kitchen until we start to make something and that can be frustrating. Having the right kitchen tools sets us up for kitchen success. Their functionality encourages us to keep cooking. The more you cook, the more tools you'll want to have on hand because they make it all so much easier. And, we'll admit it, kitchen gadgets are fun! (We love giving them as gifts too.) Here are a few essentials we really like having in our kitchens.

Good chef's knife (7 to 9 inches)

Good paring knife

Bread knife

Knife sharpener

2 large cutting boards (odor resistant and dishwasher-safe)

Kitchen shears

2 heat-safe silicone spatulas/spoons

Spatula/turner

Whisk

Metal tongs

Spider spatula/spider skimmer

Ladle

Large (2-cup) liquid measuring cup

Measuring cups for dry ingredients

Measuring spoons

Small (1½-quart) saucepan/pot

Medium (3-quart) saucepan/pot

Large stockpot

6- to 8-quart Dutch oven

6- to 8-quart slow cooker

8- to 10-inch cast iron skillet

Large stainless steel skillet

Medium stainless steel skillet

Sauté pan (flat bottom)

2 or 3 medium baking sheets

2 large rimmed (half-sheet) baking sheets

Pie dish

Springform pan

Loaf pan

Cupcake/muffin pan

Casserole dish

Oven mitts

Set of glass bowls in every size

Box grater

Microplane grater

Digital meat thermometer

Candy or deep-fry thermometer

Can opener

Vegetable peeler

Colander

Potato masher

Vegetable scrubber

Meat mallet

Cookie scooper

Immersion blender

Nutribullet/power blender

Food processor

Stand mixer

Juicer

Spotify playlists

A Spotify playlist is a collection of songs you can create on Spotify based on whatever you may like—a specific artist, a genre, a mood, or a certain vibe you want to cultivate. Using the Spotify app, you choose songs and simply click "add" to add the song to your playlist. You can create your own playlist, collaborate with friends or family on a group list, or simply enjoy any of the many Spotify-created lists. We love classical music while making soup or baking on a rainy day; classic jazz or Kelsey's Sunday Morning playlist while cooking weekend brunch; fun, low-key pop when we're entertaining family and friends; and country music grilling on a sunny day. We even found a playlist full of Italian music when we taught ourselves how to make gnocchi and pasta. There are a host of options for you to choose from. It's so fun and easy!

about the recipes

We believe in whole-body health. We believe food is nourishment for the mind, body, and soul. We believe that all foods can be enjoyed without a side of guilt or shame. And our recipes encompass that philosophy. We hope our recipes will boost your overall well-being and inspire you to cook them for yourself and those you love.

"stickers" for added love + inspiration

We've added some "extra love" in our cookbook for you too. Look for **Tradition, Complete Meal** and **Plant-Forward** stickers in the recipes, which indicate a little something extra and special for you.

tradition

The *tradition* sticker means that a particular recipe has been part of a tradition for us with family or friends. We believe our greatest nourishment and joy come from cooking and eating with loved ones. And traditions give steadiness and rhythm to life that help us feel a sense of security, normalcy, inclusion, and balance. Building traditions around our cooking and sharing meals with friends and family truly builds our well-being, helps bond us with the people we love, and provides a sense of belonging. When we include someone in our traditions, it shows them they are important to us and that we value the relationship. In addition, following family traditions reminds us to live more intentionally to feed our relationships, and in doing so, feed our whole selves. When you see a *tradition* sticker, you'll know it's part of a lot of hearts. We hope that maybe some of our recipes will inspire you to start traditions of your own that will create beautiful moments and memories for you.

complete meal

When feeding our physical self, science proves the best way is to eat with balance for consistent, long-lasting energy. A complete meal by nutritional standards includes carbs, lean protein, heart-healthy fats, and color from produce. When you see the *Complete Meal* sticker on a recipe, you don't have to worry about what else you may need to add to that meal to make it complete and satisfying. Our recipe does all of the nutritional thinking for you.

In addition, the *Complete Meal* sticker will help you become more aware of what a complete meal actually is. Awareness helps inspire all of us to keep moving in a more healthful, energized direction. We hope complete meal awareness inspires you to keep that thought process going as you plan other meals.

plant-forward

Adding even more awareness for improved health, you'll see *Plant-Forward* stickers on some of our recipes. "Plant-forward" means placing more focus on plant-based foods and making them the star of your plate. This is not the same thing as "plant-exclusive," which restricts all animal products. Animal products and proteins can still be part of your balanced plate, just think of them as more of a side dish or garnish. Unless we are food scientists or registered dietitians, it can be very confusing navigating what's in and what's out for nutritious eating. Luckily, the Peddies have Kendall in our life—she's our resident registered dietitian. And now you have her in your life too. Kendall assures us one thing we can always count on to be true is we need to eat more plants. We need color—color is life! We hope we inspire you to add more plants to your life so you can add more years to your life!

more love and inspiration ...

In addition to the stickers, some of our recipes have special bonus features that we want to make you aware of: *Sexy Slow Cooker, Gluten-Free,* and space for note-taking.

sexy slow cooker recipes

Be sure to look for the *Sexy Slow Cooker* recipes. The slow cooker is like having a friend (it's fun if you name her) who says, "Hey, I see everything you're doing and how hard you're trying; let me make dinner for you tonight." She's the pal who has dinner ready by the time you're done with work and makes it possible to entertain without a lot of time and stress.

Some people blame the slow cooker for meals that are dull, frumpy, and mushy. It's not her fault; those recipes weren't meant to come from a slow cooker. Our *Sexy Slow Cooker* recipes are fresh, fun, and flirty and were developed expressly for the slow cooker. We also think too many slow cooker recipes create a lot of dirty pots and pans before the food even makes it to the slow cooker. That's not her fault either and defeats her purpose, so we've tried to minimize that for you. Her remarkable ability to help us has made us want to help her get her sexy back!

gluten-free recipes

Sharon developed an allergy to wheat as an adult, and we had to learn to adapt. So an unintended and very exciting added bit of love in our cookbook is that every recipe is easily adaptable to be gluten-free. That may not sound like a big deal to many, but for the gluten-free community, being able to be join in when they smell something delicious cooking is everything!

Any time you see "all-purpose flour" in our recipes, know that we have also made that recipe many times with gluten-free flour, so you can confidently substitute your favorite gluten-free all-purpose flour. (We usually turn to Cup4Cup Multipurpose Flour for any all-purpose flour situations including baking. But we also use Bob's Red Mill Gluten-Free 1-to-1 Baking Flour for cakes, scones, cookies, and muffins.) Keep this in mind when seeing recipes with panko, soy, etc. You can confidently substitute GF products there too.

space for note-taking

We've included a small area on the recipes for you to write ♡ notes. A cookbook is much like a diary in that it can be a time capsule, showing family love and history within its pages. This is especially true when you take the time to write notes. Each time we use a recipe, we write down notes on how to do it better the next time or to make it even more to our liking. It's so useful to write those helpful tips right on the recipe because we never remember them the next time. It's also fun to indicate when you made first made the recipe, who you made it for, or how it made you feel because a good cookbook should never look brand-new; it should have stains and notes scattered throughout. We've also included some extra space with journaling pages in the back of the book. We hope it inspires you to pass your special notes and cookbook along to many generations to come.

everyday

recipes

that will make
you feel loved

sunshiney breakfasts

Every morning, we have a chance to start fresh. Too often, we jump right into news, emails, texts, and social media as soon as we wake up. It can exhaust us before we even step into the kitchen or walk out the door. We deserve our wellness to be intentional from the moment our eyes open. Nurturing ourselves with breakfast is a loving way to set a sunny, powerful intention for our day. Whether it's a weekend with a little more time or a busy weekday, we have some fun breakfast inspiration for you.

cookies for breakfast

ready in 30 minutes
makes 18 cookies

1 (16-ounce) package gluten-
    free cookie mix (we love
    King Arthur brand)
1 large apple, peeled,
    cored, and shredded
    (a box grater works
    fast and easy)
1 cup rolled whole grain oats
1 cup walnuts
½ cup crunchy granola
    of choice (we love
    Kind oats and honey
    with toasted coconut,
    which is gluten-free)
⅓ cup pepitas
½ cup dried cranberries
¼ cup flaxseed powder
¼ cup sunflower seeds
¼ cup black chia seeds
1 teaspoon pumpkin pie spice
½ teaspoon ground cinnamon
½ cup avocado oil
1 large egg
3 tablespoons water
1 cup dark chocolate
    chunks or chips

 **notes**

Cookies for breakfast? Doesn't that sound so fun, but like something your mom said wouldn't be a good idea? Well, she didn't meet these cookies. They're delicious, nutritious, and pretty exciting when you remember you have them! These cookies are something you can make on the weekends and have on hand all week. They're a happy, energetic way to start your day.

Preheat the oven to 350°F. Line one large or two medium cookie sheets with parchment paper.

In a large mixing bowl or stand mixer, combine all of the ingredients except the chocolate chunks, and mix until well blended. Add a little more water if needed; the dough should be sticky and heavy. Blend in the chocolate chunks.

Scoop ¼-cup portions of the dough and drop them onto the cookie sheets, placing them 2 to 3 inches apart. There's really no right or wrong shape, but a ¼ cup gives you a meaningful cookie. Bake for 15 to 18 minutes until lightly browned and desired texture is achieved. Let cool or eat warm.

Store in an airtight container at room temperature for four days or in the freezer for up to three weeks to preserve the integrity of the perfect cookie texture.

tip

The dough is very sticky, so rinse the ¼-cup scoop with water after scooping four or five cookies. It will help them fall out of the measuring cup more easily.

dutch baby with sautéed apples

ready in 35 minutes
serves 2 to 3

dutch baby

2 tablespoons
   unsalted butter

½ cup oat milk (or
   milk of choice)

3 large eggs, beaten

1 teaspoon vanilla extract

½ cup all-purpose flour
   of your choice

1 tablespoon sugar

½ teaspoon ground cinnamon

sautéed apple topping

2 tablespoons
   unsalted butter

2 large apples (we like
   to use Honeycrisp),
   peeled and sliced thin

½ teaspoon ground cinnamon

¼ teaspoon ground nutmeg

½ cup maple syrup
   (more if desired)

+ added yum:
   Powdered sugar for
   finishing on top

Do you believe in creating magic just to impress and delight yourself? You will feel like a magician as you take your Dutch baby out of the oven. It's like a cross between a pancake, crepe, and popover that rises high! Poof! It's so cute and comforting. Create this magic for yourself; it's special, and so are you. There will be enough to share—but only if you want to!

Preheat the oven to 425°F.

for the dutch baby

Place the butter in a size 8 (about 10-inch) cast iron skillet and put the pan in the heating oven. When the butter has melted, evenly distribute it over the bottom of the pan.

In a large mixing bowl, combine the milk, eggs, and vanilla. Whisk in the flour, sugar, and cinnamon until well combined.

Pour the batter into the hot, buttered skillet. Return to the oven and bake for about 15 minutes or until the pancake is puffed and golden brown.

for the topping

While the Dutch baby pancake is baking, melt the butter in a medium skillet over medium heat.

Add the apple slices and sauté for 3 to 4 minutes until browned. Add the cinnamon and nutmeg and stir to coat the apples with the spices. Pour in the maple syrup and cook until warmed. Let the topping rest until the Dutch baby is done.

Right before serving, spoon the apple topping all over the Dutch baby. **+ added yum:** Finish with a sprinkling of powdered sugar.

tip

First time making: Peel and slice apples before beginning anything. It will keep you from rushing the topping while the Dutch baby is baking.

chocolate + chocolate chip zucchini muffins

ready in 40 minutes
makes 12 muffins

1 cup all-purpose
  flour of choice
½ cup good cocoa powder
1 teaspoon baking soda
½ teaspoon kosher salt
2 large eggs
¼ cup avocado oil
¼ cup unsalted butter,
  melted and cooled
¾ cup packed dark
  brown sugar
1½ teaspoons pure
  vanilla extract
1½ cups packed shredded
  zucchini (1 or 2 zucchini)
2 cups dark chocolate chips

 **notes**

Muffins are a fast and happy breakfast! We started making these muffins for Cami when she was growing up. She liked to sleep until the last possible moment before getting ready for school and was willing to skip breakfast for a couple of extra zzz's. These were a great grab-and-go to ensure she started her day with breakfast. They have become a family favorite.

Preheat the oven to 350°F. Grease the cups of a standard 12-cup muffin pan or line with cupcake liners.

In a medium bowl, combine the flour, cocoa powder, baking soda, and salt. In a stand mixer or large bowl, mix the eggs, oil, butter, brown sugar, and vanilla.

With the mixer on low, slowly add the dry ingredients to the wet, mixing well. Stir in the shredded zucchini and 1½ cups of the chocolate chips.

Pour batter into the prepared muffin cups to about two-thirds full. Sprinkle the remaining ½ cup chocolate chips on the tops.

Bake for 20 to 23 minutes until a toothpick inserted into the center of a muffin comes out mostly clean and not goopy. (However, there may be some melted chocolate chips on the toothpick.)

brunchy baguette bar inspo

ready in 30 minutes
serves 6

1 large French baguette,
   sliced thin (easier
   to bite through)
Extra-virgin olive oil,
   for drizzling
Toppings of choice (our
   favorites: cream cheese
   spreads of different
   flavors, truffle goat
   cheese, soft-boiled eggs,
   salmon, avocado slices,
   green peas, tomato slices,
   blanched asparagus,
   radishes, chives,
   roasted beets, zoodles,
   arugula, microgreens,
   edible flowers, etc.)

 **notes**

A beautiful brunch baguette bar with a fresh, sliced baguette and all kinds of delicious spreads and toppings is unique, delicious, and easy entertaining for a girlie brunch. (But shhh: Guys love this baguette bar, too!) You can do all of your cutting and prepping the day before. Invite your guests to pick and choose from among the bountiful choices. It's so fun to see everyone's creative combinations.

And why not set up a mimosa bar with pretty champagne glasses next to the baguette bar for a colorful, festive spread?

Preheat the oven to 350°F.

Drizzle each slice of baguette with olive oil. Spread out the slices on a baking sheet and toast in the oven just until the slices are slightly crunchy, about 1 or 2 minutes.

Set up a pretty board with your favorite cheese spreads and toppings. Let your brunch guests create something beautiful and delicious!

fall-in-love granola

ready in 1 hour, 15 minutes
serves 8 to 12

5 cups rolled oats
1 cup extra-virgin olive oil
½ cup maple syrup
½ cup honey
1 cup pecan pieces
½ cup walnut pieces
½ cup chia seeds
½ cup pumpkin seeds
½ cup sesame seeds
½ cup uncooked quinoa,
    rinsed well
1 teaspoon pumpkin pie spice
½ teaspoon ground cinnamon
½ teaspoon kosher salt
1 cup raisins or dried
    fruits of choice

+ added yum:
    Dark chocolate chunks,
    Greek vanilla yogurt

 **notes**

Fall brings an undeniable cozy feeling to our souls and doesn't need to be your favorite season to appreciate the rich, copper hues that blanket the landscape—or the perfume of warm spices that imbue our favorite foods. This nutrition-packed granola will help you feel warm and cozy in any season. The crunch and flavors are an energizing start for whatever comes your way. We love it on top of low-fat Greek yogurt.

Preheat the oven 350°F. Line a large baking sheet with parchment paper.

In a large bowl, toss the oats, olive oil, maple syrup, and honey to combine well. Spread out evenly on the prepared baking sheet. Bake for 25 minutes, but keep an eye on it so the edges don't burn. If they start getting dark, stir and flip as needed to move the outside parts into the center, and then spread everything back out.

Meanwhile, in the same bowl, mix the pecans, walnuts, chia seeds, pumpkin seeds, sesame seeds, quinoa, pumpkin spice, cinnamon, and salt and combine well.

After the granola has baked, add the nut mixture and move everything around the baking sheet to incorporate evenly. Then, spread out the granola and bake for 15 to 20 minutes longer or until golden brown. We're looking for it to turn crunchy and golden but not burned. Let cool for 30 minutes.

Once the granola has cooled, add the raisins or other dried fruit.

+ added yum: Serve with Greek yogurt if you like. And for a real treat, add chocolate chunks to the mix.

Store in Mason jars or airtight plastic containers at room temperature for up to 10 days.

tip

Every oven is different, so keep an eye on the process to prevent burned edges.

maple-glazed apple scones

ready in 55 minutes
makes 8 scones

2 cups all-purpose flour

6 tablespoons granulated
sugar + more for sprinkling

2½ teaspoons baking powder

1 teaspoon ground cinnamon

Pinch of kosher salt

½ cup (1 stick) unsalted
butter, frozen

½ cup heavy cream +
2 tablespoons, divided

1 large egg

1½ teaspoons pure
vanilla extract

1 cup shredded, peeled
apple (about 1 medium
apple; we love Honeycrisp
for this recipe)

gooey maple glaze

2 tablespoons unsalted
butter, melted

1 cup powdered sugar

¼ cup pure maple syrup

1 to 2 teaspoons maple
extract (optional, for
deeper maple flavor)

Why do we love a great coffee shop? It's because, with their rich aroma of coffee and yummy baked breakfast goods, it has a warm and inviting environment. And the very best have a special buzz that just seems to promote both creativity and relaxation at the same time. Some people say they get some of their best work done at coffee shops. We love recreating a coffee house vibe for ourselves at home. Nothing does it better than a crunchy, gooey, glazed scone, a fresh pot of coffee, and a jazzy coffee house playlist. Try this combo at home and you'll create something very special for yourself. What will you name your coffee house?

In a large bowl, whisk together the flour, granulated sugar, baking powder, cinnamon, and salt. Using a box grater, grate the frozen butter directly into the flour mixture; do this quickly, so the butter doesn't melt. Using two forks, combine the butter and flour until it all comes together and looks like a bunch of crumbs. Don't use your hands yet; you want to keep the dough cold and hands will warm it up too fast.

In a small bowl, whisk ½ cup of the cream with the egg and vanilla. Add to the flour mixture and combine well again with forks. Add the shredded apple and combine well with forks until all the flour mixture is worked in. Now, using your hands, quickly mix everything until it is moist and firming together. Set the dough on parchment paper and form into a disc about 8 inches in diameter. Wrap in parchment and refrigerate for 15 to 20 minutes.

Preheat the oven to 400°F and line a baking sheet with parchment paper while the scones are chillin'.

Lightly dust a chef's knife or bench scraper with flour. Use the knife or scraper to cut the dough disc into eight triangles, like a pizza pie, and place on the prepared baking sheet. Give them room to spread. Brush the cut scones with the remaining 2 tablespoons cream and sprinkle with a little granulated sugar. Bake for 23 to 25 minutes or until golden brown.

make the maple glaze

While the scones cool, mix the melted butter, powdered sugar, and maple syrup in a small bowl. If you're adding maple extract, add 1 teaspoon at a time for desired maple flavor.

Place the cooled scones on a serving plate and drizzle with your yummy maple glaze!

tips

- It's important to keep the butter and dough cold so your scones don't melt out of shape while they bake.
- To freeze the baked scones: Wrap the *unglazed*, cooled scones in parchment paper and freeze in a resealable plastic freezer bag for up to three weeks. When you're ready, let them thaw on the counter for two hours or overnight in the refrigerator. Reheat on a baking sheet in a 325°F oven for about 10 minutes. Add your glaze before serving.
- If you have Spotify, search "coffee house playlists" and find one that speaks to you—or create your own!

♡ **notes**

gooey, glazed lemon + blueberry scones

ready in 55 minutes
makes 8 scones

2 cups all-purpose flour
2½ teaspoons baking powder
6 tablespoons granulated
    sugar + more for sprinkling
Grated zest of 1 lemon
Pinch of kosher salt
½ cup (1 stick) unsalted
    butter, frozen
½ cup heavy cream
    + 2 tablespoons, divided
1 large egg
2 teaspoons pure
    vanilla extract
1 cup blueberries

gooey lemon glaze

1½ cups powdered sugar
Juice of 1 lemon

Whether you're creating your own cool coffee house vibe at home (and these will!) or wanting to gift a care basket of delicious treats, perfecting a couple of scone recipes is a beautiful thing. Making from scratch may be a little more work than opening a box of store-bought scones, but these freeze and rewarm so well! It may sound like an exaggeration, but having fresh scones on hand is life-changing. It brings heartwarming care to your life! We gave you a fall apple scone recipe, so here's a springy/summer one as well. They are scrumptious!

In a large bowl, whisk together the flour, baking powder, granulated sugar, lemon zest, and salt. Using a box grater, quickly grate the frozen butter into the flour mixture. Using two forks, combine the butter and flour mixture until it comes together and looks like a bunch of crumbs. Don't use your hands yet; you want to keep the dough cold and hands will warm it up too fast.

In a small bowl, whisk together ½ cup of the cream, the egg, and vanilla. Add to the flour mixture and combine well with forks. Add the blueberries and toss around lightly with forks to combine well.

Now, using your hands, quickly mix everything until the dough is moist and holding together. Set the dough on parchment paper and form into a disc about 8 inches in diameter. Wrap in parchment and refrigerate for 15 to 20 minutes.

Preheat the oven to 400°F and line a baking sheet with parchment paper while the dough is chillin'.

Lightly flour a chef's knife or bench scraper and use to cut the dough disc into 8 triangles, like a pizza pie. Place the scones on the prepared baking sheet, giving them room to spread out. Brush the cut scones with the remaining 2 tablespoons cream and sprinkle with a little granulated sugar. Bake for 23 to 25 minutes or until golden brown.

make the lemon glaze

While scones are cooling, mix the powdered sugar and lemon juice in a small bowl.

Place the cooled scones on a serving plate and drizzle with the lemon glaze.

tips

- It's important to keep the butter and dough cold so your scones don't melt out of shape while they bake.
- To freeze the baked scones: Wrap the *unglazed*, cooled scones in parchment paper and freeze in a resealable plastic freezer bag for up to three weeks. When you're ready, let them thaw on the counter for two hours or overnight in the refrigerator. Reheat on a baking sheet in a 325°F oven for about 10 minutes. Add your glaze before serving.

 **notes**

veggie lovers' breakfast hash

ready in 45 minutes

serves 3 to 4

A greasy diner hash is a favorite for many but doesn't always leave our bodies feeling so good afterward. You don't have to be a vegetarian to fall in love with this savory, colorful hash filled with gorgeous veggies. It's delicious, nutritious, comforting, and will set your body up to feel agreeable and powerful!

1½ cups cubed sweet potato

1½ cups cubed gold potatoes

2 tablespoons
    unsalted butter

1 tablespoon extra-virgin
    olive oil

1 red bell pepper, diced small

1 leek, cut in half, rinsed
    well, and sliced thin
    (use all white parts and
    tender parts of green)

1 shallot, cut in half
    and sliced thin

1 cup Tuscan kale cut
    into ribbons

1 cup baby spinach

½ teaspoon ground
    turmeric (optional)

⅛ teaspoon ground
    cumin (optional)

½ cup fresh herbs of choice
    (sage, basil, oregano,
    and/or parsley)

+ added yum:
    ½ cup feta cheese

Place the sweet potatoes and gold potatoes in a glass bowl. Cover tightly with plastic wrap/cellophane and microwave for 5 minutes or until softened and cooked through.

Heat the butter and olive oil in a large skillet over medium heat. Add the pepper, leek, and shallot and sauté until soft, about 10 minutes. Add the potatoes and cook for 10 minutes or until the potatoes crisp and start taking on color. Add the kale, spinach, turmeric, cumin, and herbs and cook until the kale is softened, about 2 minutes.

+ added yum: Sprinkle with feta cheese before serving.

tips

- You can use any kind of potato. Sometimes we use the mini tri colors.
- You can leave out the warm spices depending on the preference of your family; it's still delicious.
- Make extra—it's a great quick breakfast you can heat up in the microwave all week. Add a fried or poached egg on top for a boost of protein.

 **notes**

perfect pumpkin bread

tradition ♥

ready in 1 hour, 20 minutes
makes 2 loaves

3 cups all-purpose flour
1 tablespoon ground
　　cinnamon
1 teaspoon kosher salt
1 teaspoon baking soda
½ teaspoon baking powder
3 large eggs
1 cup vegetable oil
2 cups sugar
1 tablespoon vanilla extract
1½ cups canned pumpkin
　　(from a 15-ounce can)
½ cup canned crushed
　　pineapple, drained

ⓥ **notes**

This bread is delightful and delectable with a cup of coffee or tea any morning. We also serve it with our Curried Apple + Butternut Squash Friendship Soup (page 66). They are like friends who make you feel warm, safe, and loved. Truly a match made in heaven.

Preheat the oven 350°F. Grease and flour two standard loaf pans (or see Tip below).

In a medium bowl, combine the flour, cinnamon, salt, baking soda, and baking powder.

In a stand mixer or large bowl, beat the eggs. Add the oil, sugar, and vanilla and blend well. Add the pumpkin and pineapple and blend well. Slowly add the flour mixture to the wet ingredients, mixing well.

Divide the batter between the prepared pans. Bake for 1 hour or until toothpick comes out clean.

tip

The breads can be baked in any baking dish with a capacity of 4 to 6 cups. There are many pumpkin-shaped pans available online if you want that shape.

scratch-made biscuits

tradition

ready in 25 minutes
makes 8 biscuits

¾ cup (1½ sticks) very
    cold unsalted butter
3 cups all-purpose
    flour of choice
3 tablespoons sugar
4 teaspoons baking powder
½ teaspoon cream of tartar
½ teaspoon kosher salt
1 large egg
1 cup milk of choice
1 tablespoon unsalted butter,
    melted, for topping
Southern Sausage Gravy
    (recipe follows), optional

Biscuit love in our family definitely stems from our Mississippi Caldwell roots. We all believe that no matter what kind of bread or trendy breakfasts enter the universe, none can ever surpass the reliability, deliciousness, and love of a homemade, crunchy, buttery biscuit! Whether the biscuit wants a little soak in a gravy hot tub (such a funny expression), stuffed as a sammie, or just wants us to spread some delicious jam on it, it's always ready and willing to hug us however we want. Sure, making biscuits from scratch isn't as easy as cracking open a biscuit tube from the store, but these are still quick, easy to whip up, and totally worth it! They freeze and heat up so well for future use too.

Preheat the oven to 450°F. Line a baking sheet with parchment paper.

Use a box grater to grate the butter into pieces; put in the freezer while starting the dough.

Combine the flour, sugar, baking powder, cream of tartar, and salt in a large bowl. In a medium bowl, whisk together the egg and milk.

Add the cold grated butter to the dry ingredients. Without handling the dough too much, toss the butter around in the flour, keeping the butter in pieces throughout the blending process as much as you can. Add the egg and milk mixture and continue to blend to start forming the dough. Use a fork to keep blending all the ingredients. Add a bit more milk if needed and use your hands, but don't overwork. You should be able to pinch some of the dough so it holds together.

To form the biscuits, pinch off about one-eighth of the dough (between the size of a golf ball and a tennis ball). Roll into a ball and then softly mash it between your hands to form a biscuit shape that is about 1-inch thick. Give the sides a few soft squeezes as you rotate it around in your hand to build your desired shape.

Place each on the prepared baking sheet. Spoon a little of the melted butter on top of each biscuit to help brown the tops.

Bake for 10 to 15 minutes until nicely golden brown on top. Serve simply with butter, jam, or honey. If you want to take it to the next level, drop them in a hot tub of our Southern Sausage Gravy (next page), or check out our Biscuit Sammies Inspo (page 38).

notes

tips

- The most important tip is to use very cold butter, egg, and milk!
- To freeze biscuits, wrap them in parchment paper, place in a resealable plastic freezer bag, and freeze for up to three weeks. Thaw in the refrigerator overnight, on the counter for two hours, or in the microwave for 30 to 45 seconds.

southern sausage gravy

tradition ♥

**ready in 20 minutes
serves 4 to 6**

1 (16-ounce) roll of Jimmy
   Dean premium pork
   sausage (there's
   nothing like it)
¾ cup all-purpose flour
Fresh cracked pepper
4 cups milk

 **notes**

A crunchy biscuit, sitting in a hot tub of piping hot, peppery, sausage gravy ... omg! Biscuits and gravy is a Southern classic with roots back to the Revolutionary War. It was an inexpensive way to provide a hearty breakfast for many—and still is. Our Mississippi family has been making this dish for generations. Sharon's dad taught her how to make it when she was just a kid. Sometimes, we crave those cozy or nostalgic dishes that feed our soul. They make us feel comforted, safe, and loved because of the family and beautiful memories attached to them. Not everything we eat always has to provide the highest nutritional value possible in one dish; at times, we have to care for our whole being—mind, body, and soul. This is good ole Southern comfort food that fits into a category we like to call "soul food."

Heat a cast iron skillet or large sauté pan over medium-high heat. Crumble in the sausage meat and spread out. Let the sausage sit and cook for a bit before you start moving it around (the dark crispy bits are everything!). Stir until cooked through.

Sprinkle in the flour and add six good twists from your black pepper grinder. Mix well with the sausage and let the flour brown well, about 2 minutes, but don't let it burn.

Add the milk and bring to a boil. Once a slow boil begins, reduce the heat and cook until it thickens into a gravy, 5 to 10 minutes. Give the gravy another good dose of pepper, stir, and spoon over fresh biscuits or into a bowl and drop the biscuit in—whichever is your style!

biscuit sammies inspo:
meat, egg + cheese biscuits

**ready in 5 minutes
(with premade
biscuits and meat)**
serves 1

1 Scratch-Made Biscuit
(page 34), cut in half
1 egg
1 slice of cheese
Meat and/or veggies
of choice
Personalize it how you love it!

♡ **notes**

This falls into inspiration more than recipe—but sometimes that's all we need. We know we've all dragged ourselves out for a good ole biscuit sandwich from a drive-thru at some point in our lives, but you get to stay at home in your jammies for this one. Next time you make a batch of our scratch biscuits, be sure to freeze a few extras after baking. You'll be able to whip up one of these biscuit sammies on the quick when you're craving one.

Eggs: fried or scrambled?

Cheese: your favorite (or two favorites! Who doesn't want to add more cheese?!)

Meat: bacon? sausage? brisket? maybe tofu or veggies? All work well!

sexy slow cooker oatmeal board

ready in 20 minutes

serves 8

3 cups rolled oats (see Tip)

6 cups hot water

Topping board ideas:

    brown sugar, raisins,

    dried apricots,

    applesauce, bananas,

    blueberries, strawberries,

    assorted nuts, chia

    seeds, pumpkin seeds,

    sesame seeds

 **notes**

We have a little retreat in the mountains and often have a house full of visitors. People get up and eat at different times, so this is a loving, welcoming way to have a nutritious breakfast ready and waiting for guests, regardless of their sleep schedule. It looks so pretty and inviting, and some people are so enthusiastic— they act like they're making an ice cream sundae instead of a bowl of oatmeal! Whether you're going on a hike or having some friends over for an early football game, this is another impressive, stress-free way to entertain. Our sexy slow cooker friend delivers once again!

Mix the oats with the hot water in the slow cooker. Cook on high for 15 minutes. Move the setting to low to keep oatmeal warm for to 2 to 3 hours.

While the oatmeal is cooking, assemble and set out the toppings for a colorful board filled with fun and healthy toppings.

tip

We love Bob's Red Mill Quick Cooking Steel Cut Oats for this. The texture holds well while staying warm in the slow cooker.

the camwich

complete
meal

ready in 5 to 6 minutes

serves 1

1 tablespoon avocado
or olive oil

1 egg, beaten

2 slices extra seedy
wheat bread

¼ cup shredded
cheddar cheese

Kosher salt and black
pepper to taste

1 cup baby spinach

 **notes**

Is an egg sandwich something anyone really needs a recipe for? No, probably not. Is it something we hope will inspire you to make it for yourself? Yes, and here's why: A wheaty, seedy breakfast sandwich stuffed with egg, cheese, and spinach is a healthful, wonderful way to start your day. We call it the Camwich because it's one of the very first things little Cami learned to cook all by herself. Served with a side of fruit or a glass of fresh-pressed OJ, it was a great introduction to preparing a complete and balanced meal. This is quick, easy, nutritious, and delicious at any age! Let's get some more Camwiches in your life ;)

Heat the oil in a small skillet over medium heat. Add the beaten egg and let it sit for 2 to 3 minutes without stirring. Toast the bread while the egg is cooking.

Use a rubber spatula to loosen underneath the edges of the egg, then carefully flip the egg over and add the cheese. Still using the spatula, fold in the sides to make a square. Season with salt and pepper to taste.

Place the spinach on the toast, then top with the cheesy egg. Cut sideways to make 2 triangles.

Go snuggle on the couch and enjoy your Camwich with a glass of fresh-squeezed orange juice!

warm maple walnut bread

tradition ♥

ready in 1 hour, 15 minutes
serves 8

2 cups all-purpose flour

1 cup sugar

1 tablespoon baking powder

1 teaspoon kosher salt

1 cup oat milk (or other
    milk of choice)

1 large egg, well beaten

3 tablespoons maple
    flavoring

Heaping cup walnut pieces

 **notes**

Nothing says it must be Christmas morning in our house like the warm, maple-y smells of this delicious, buttery bread. Our tradition is to prep the dry ingredients on Christmas Eve. Then, Christmas morning, we mix in the wet ingredients as soon as we wake up, pop it into the oven—and open presents while the bread bakes. Christmas carols in the background and aroma of this delicious bread wafting in the forefront fill our hearts with simple joy.

Preheat the oven to 350°F. Grease a standard loaf pan with cooking spray.

Blend the flour, sugar, baking powder, and salt in a bowl. In a stand mixer, combine the milk, egg, and maple flavoring and mix well. Slowly mix in the flour mixture.

Pour into prepared loaf pan. Bake for 1 hour or until toothpick comes out clean.

smart smoothies

Throughout any given day, there are many times we could use a little more motivation, focus, and strength. A smart smoothie is a supportive tool to help us with just that! Each smoothie here—packed with fruits and vegetables and loaded with antioxidants and fiber—aid in digestion, improve our brainpower, boost our mood, and help support our immunity. We hope these recipes (all of them are registered dietitian-approved) inspire more smoothies in your life.

blueberry + beet smoothie

plant forward

ready in 5 minutes

serves 1

¼ cup frozen peeled beets
    (raw or cooked, see Tips)
¾ cup frozen blueberries
½ cup fresh baby spinach
¼ cup Greek yogurt
¼ cup pressed OJ
1 teaspoon flax seeds
½ cup ice

 **notes**

This has been Sharon's favorite breakfast smoothie for years. She loves the earthiness of the beets and spinach balanced with sweet liveliness from the OJ and blueberries. It wakes up her tastebuds and feels like sunshine to her body. Packed with fiber, antioxidants, and a punch of protein from Greek yogurt and flax seeds, the smoothie is great any time—but is an especially positive, supercharged way to start the day! Sharon insists on using frozen beets and berries because she likes her smoothies to have a good slush.

Add all ingredients to a blender, blend to desired texture, and enjoy!

tips

• The frozen berries and beets are what make a thick, slushy smoothie.
• Plan ahead and peel, cube, and freeze raw beets or buy cooked beets in the refrigerated produce section of most supermarkets, then cube and freeze them. Either way tastes great.

cheery chard + cherry smoothie

plant forward

ready in 5 minutes

serves 1

2 Swiss chard leaves, washed

1 cup frozen dark cherries

2 stalks celery, washed

¼ cup water

¼ cup ice cubes

Such a good-friend smoothie! The deep, rich, black cherry flavor combined with the crisp taste of greens feels like a friendly supercharge to your senses. It has Swiss chard for vitamin K (for proper blood clotting), cherries for vitamin C (maintains proper immune function and collagen formation), and celery for insoluble fiber (helps you feel fuller longer and aids in digestion).

Add all ingredients to a blender, blend to desired texture, and enjoy!

 **notes**

green matcha calming energy smoothie

plant
forward

ready in 5 minutes
serves 1

½ cup vanilla Greek yogurt

½ cup cashew milk, or
    milk of choice

1 cup fresh baby spinach

¼ avocado

1½ teaspoons matcha
    powder

½ teaspoon honey

½ cup ice

This smoothie is the perfect mid-morning or early afternoon pick-me-up. It provides our bodies with carbs, protein, and heart-healthy fats. Earthy with a touch of sweetness, it provides a "calm energy" because it has both caffeine (for energy) and a compound called L-theanine, known to have relaxation properties. We love it so matcha!

Add all ingredients to a blender, blend to desired texture, and enjoy!

 **notes**

orange is the new pink smoothie

plant forward

ready in 5 minutes
serves 1

½ cup chopped carrot
   (about 1 carrot)
1 small apple (or ½ large
   apple), peeled and cored
1 Cutie orange (or ½ of a
   regular orange), peeled
¼ cup frozen peaches
¼ teaspoon grated
   fresh ginger
   (about pinkie tip size)
¼ teaspoon ground turmeric
Small pinch black pepper
½ cup cashew milk,
   or milk of choice

Think Dreamsicle/Creamsicle with a sassy little zip! This beautiful smoothie makes you feel beautiful drinking it! It's packed with vitamin A and vitamin C, both of which have antioxidant properties. Turmeric alone helps reduce inflammation, but the effect is enhanced by eating it with black pepper.

Add all ingredients to a blender, blend to desired texture, and enjoy!

♡ **notes**

peanut butter + banana smoothie

ready in 5 minutes

serves 1

½ cup milk of choice

1 frozen banana

1 tablespoon natural
   peanut butter or nut
   butter of choice

1½ teaspoons chia seeds

Ice or additional milk
   to achieve desired
   consistency

Kendall's favorite post-workout treat is a creamy, rich, and satisfying smoothie that provides the body with the carbs and protein it needs to recover after exercise. The chia seeds add a boost of plant-based protein and heart-healthy fatty acids.

Add all ingredients to a blender, blend to desired texture, and enjoy!

 **notes**

soothing, soulful SOUPS

A delicious bowl of soup can feel like a warm hug and a dose of sunshine. We live in the Pacific Northwest where it rains seven months of the year, so it's safe to say we live with a chill n our bones. When we come in from the rain, we're always looking for coffee, tea, or soup to warm us up! Consequently, we've built a nice repertoire of comforting, nutritious soups that feel so good to the soul. It was hard for us to choose which ones would make the cut, but we think you'll agree they all will feel like a warm hug.

carrot + orange + ginger soup

plant forward

ready in 35 minutes

serves 4 to 5

3 tablespoons
    unsalted butter
1 medium yellow
    onion, chopped
2 tablespoons grated
    fresh ginger
6 cups chicken broth
2 pounds carrots, peeled
    and shredded or
    sliced very thinly
2 cups freshly squeezed
    orange juice
1 cup heavy whipping cream
Kosher salt and freshly
    ground black
    pepper to taste

This soup is a bright bowl of sunshine that we love making when skies are gray! The sunny flavors and brilliant color will make this one of your new favorite, good-mood foods. It's also a valuable immune booster because it's packed with vitamins A and C.

Melt the butter in a stockpot over medium heat. Add the onion and ginger and sauté until the onion is softened. Add the broth and carrots and bring to a simmer. Cover and simmer for 25 minutes or until everything is very soft. Remove from heat.

With an immersion blender, puree the soup until smooth. Add the orange juice and puree until mixed thoroughly. Drop in the cream and puree until desired texture. Add salt and pepper to taste. Serve warm.

tips

- If you're in a hurry, you can use pre-shredded carrots to make the process move more quickly.
- You may want to add more broth or more OJ to get your desired texture and flavor.

 **notes**

could-use-a-hug chicken noodle soup

complete meal

ready in 40 minutes

serves 6

2 tablespoons extra-virgin
olive oil

2 tablespoons
unsalted butter

5 large carrots, peeled
and thickly sliced
on the diagonal

5 stalks celery, cut into
in ½-inch pieces

1 large sweet yellow onion,
finely chopped

3 cloves fresh garlic,
smashed, peeled,
and chopped

3 tablespoons chopped
fresh parsley

1 tablespoon finely chopped
fresh rosemary

1 tablespoon chopped
fresh oregano leaves

½ teaspoon freshly
ground black pepper

1 bay leaf

8 cups chicken broth

1 (8-ounce) package brown
rice noodles used for
pad Thai, broken in half

3 cups shredded chicken (we
love rotisserie chicken
for this recipe; see Tip)

Everyone should have a really good chicken noodle soup recipe in their back pocket. Life is beautiful, but it is also hard, and sometimes we need to simply nurture ourselves. A cozy, warm bowl of homemade chicken noodle soup is a perfect way to show ourselves—and our loved ones—some love and care. It's like love and a warm hug in a bowl.

In a large soup pot or Dutch oven, heat the oil and butter over medium-high heat. Reduce heat to medium and carefully add the carrots, celery, and onion. Sauté until the veggies begin to soften, about 5 minutes. Add the garlic, parsley, rosemary, oregano, pepper, and bay leaf and cook for 1 to 2 minutes.

Add the broth, increase the heat to medium-high, and bring to a simmer. Add the noodles and simmer for 5 minutes. Reduce the heat and simmer until noodles are tender, about 10 minutes. Add the chicken and simmer about 3 minutes or until the chicken is warmed through. Remove the bay leaf before serving.

tip

To shred the rotisserie chicken, separate the meat from the skin and bones and pull into bite-size strands and pieces. We like to leave the strands a little thick.

 **notes**

creamy garlic + kale soup with pancetta

complete meal

ready in 1 hour, 15 minutes

serves 4

4 heads garlic

3 tablespoons extra-virgin
olive oil, divided

2 (5- to 6-ounce) packages
diced pancetta

1 yellow sweet onion,
finely chopped

4 cups chicken broth

2 cups Tuscan kale ribbons
(thick stems removed)

⅔ cup grated Parmesan
cheese

1 cup heavy cream

Kosher salt and freshly
ground black pepper

+ added yum:
Thinly sliced French
baguette and shredded
Gruyère cheese

We like serving this elegant soup to friends for an intimate lunch, at book club meetings, and anywhere else we can show it off! It's special and unique and will make you feel so cheffy. The sweet, roasted garlic coupled with creamy Parmesan makes it both comforting and decadent. And the beautiful dark green kale ribbons and crispy pancetta are like little floating treasures. For more decadence, top with rustic, toasted French bread with melted Gruyère. The dunk, the crunch, the silkiness—so scrumptious!

Preheat the oven to 350°F.

Cut through the tops of the heads of garlic just enough to expose the cloves. Drizzle 2 tablespoons of the olive oil across all exposed cloves. Wrap each bulb entirely, with the cut side facing up, separately in foil and place on a baking sheet. Roast for 45 minutes until the garlic is soft. Let cool completely, then press the skins to drop the pulp into a small bowl (see Tips) and set aside.

Heat the remaining 1 tablespoon olive oil in a large soup pot over medium heat. Add the diced pancetta and cook until crispy, about 5 minutes. With a slotted spoon, remove pancetta and set aside. Discard all but 1 tablespoon of the oil from the pan.

Reheat the oil over medium heat. Add the onions and cook until they start to caramelize. Add the garlic pulp and the broth and stir well. Bring to a simmer. Remove from heat and use an immersion blender to purée the soup until smooth.

Return the pot to medium heat. Add the kale ribbons and Parmesan cheese and simmer until the kale is tender, 1 to 2 minutes. Add the cream and keep simmering until heated through. Season to taste with salt and pepper. Ladle into soup bowls and sprinkle the pancetta evenly over each serving.

+ added yum: Toast baguette slices with melted Gruyère cheese for dunking! Here's how: Arrange baguette slices on a foil-lined baking sheet. Drizzle a small amount of olive oil on one side of each slice. Place under the broiler for about a minute. Flip them over, sprinkle on grated Gruyère, and broil for 1 more minute or until bubbly and melted (watch carefully).

tips

- Roasting the garlic takes time, but the soup comes together pretty quickly after that. The garlic can be roasted ahead of time and stored in closed container in the refrigerator for up to one week.
- When squeezing the garlic bulbs after roasting, start from the bottom and keep turning and squeezing each side over a bowl to get out all the pulp.

 **notes**

curried apple + butternut squash friendship soup

ready in 1 hour
serves 4 to 5

4 teaspoons unsalted butter

1 large yellow onion,
    finely chopped

3 to 4 teaspoons curry
    powder (you decide
    your heat level)

3 cups chicken broth
    (have more on hand
    to adjust texture)

2 butternut squash, peeled,
    cored, and chopped into
    1-inch pieces (4 to 5 cups)

3 Honeycrisp (or your
    favorite) apples, peeled,
    cored, and chopped

1 cup apple juice or cider

+ added yum:
    Mascarpone cheese
    or cream cheese

I first made this soup recipe about 26 years ago. We'd just moved to Connecticut for Tom's job. He had some work friends, but I didn't know a soul outside of him and Kelsey (Kendall was on the way). We joined a newcomers' cooking and dinner group so I could make some friends. I was assigned this soup at the first dinner; I had no idea what a butternut squash even looked like, never mind know how to cut or peel it or what parts to use! This was before the internet, so it was actually kind of comical, but it was an adventure and, surprisingly, the soup turned out absolutely delicious.

We were only in Connecticut for a couple of years, and since then I've had many other chances to make new friends. I've found the best way is to invite people into my home, cook for them, and break bread together.

When we moved to Oregon, I started a Fall Friendship Luncheon tradition where I celebrate all my wonderful friends by serving this beautiful soup, along with our Perfect Pumpkin Bread (page 32). Life got busy so I stopped doing them, but each time I make a batch of the soup, I fill a few Mason jars and drop them off to special friends to let them know I cherish them.

The soup is warm, sweet, and inviting and I'd like to think it's an extension of the kind of friend that I value being. I have thanked it many times over the years because, together, we've made some beautiful friendships. I've made the recipe more of my own over the years for a little more mass appeal—a little less curry spice, a little more apple, and a smoother texture!

—Sharon

In a large soup pot, melt the butter over medium heat. Stir in the onions and curry powder, cover, and cook over low heat until onions are translucent and soft, 10 to 12 minutes.

Add the broth, squash, and apples, and bring to a boil. Reduce the heat and simmer, partially covered, until the squash and apples are very tender, about 30 minutes.

Remove from heat. With an immersion blender, puree the soup until very smooth. Stir in the apple juice and continue to blend to desired consistency.

+ added yum: Swirl mascarpone or cream cheese into the hot soup and top with fresh parsley.

♡ **notes**

grilled corn, corn, corn chicken chowder

complete meal

ready in 45 minutes
serves 4 to 5

Okay, this soup almost didn't make the cookbook because we weren't sure it was unique enough, but it's Cami's favorite and she thought we would be crazy to exclude it. It's really a basic chowder at its core, but in its defense, it's so yummy you'll want it in your regular dinner rotation. We guess this recipe is a good life lesson: Not everything has to be glamorous and shiny to be special. Sometimes familiar, simple, unpretentious, and comfortably reliable is just the kind of special we need.

The recipe is a corn lover's dream. We load it up with corn. Not just any corn, but grilled sweet corn. Of course, you can use frozen and it works well (you'll need about 4½ cups or two 10-ounce packages), but if you want to experience it at the top of its game, use grilled fresh corn and a lot of it!

6 ears fresh corn, husked

4 tablespoons extra-virgin
 olive oil, divided

2 tablespoons
 unsalted butter

1 medium sweet yellow
 onion, diced

6 carrots, peeled and cut
 into ¼-inch-thick discs

4 cloves fresh garlic,
 smashed, peeled,
 and minced

½ teaspoon thyme leaves

¼ cup cornstarch

2 tablespoons Old Bay
 seasoning

6 cups chicken broth

30 small creamer gold
 potatoes, halved

2 bay leaves

1 rotisserie chicken, meat
 pulled off and cut into
 bite-sized pieces

1 (12-ounce) can
 evaporated milk

+ added yum:
 Cheddar cheese

 **notes**

Heat a grill to medium-high heat. Brush the corn with 2 tablespoons of olive oil and grill for 6 to 8 minutes until the kernels are soft, dark yellow, and lightly charred. Let cool slightly. Place a clean kitchen towel on a baking sheet. Standing one ear of corn on the towel, use a sharp knife to cut off the kernels, close to the cob to get full clumps of corn. Repeat to cut the corn from all six ears. Lift the towel and dump the corn into a bowl and set aside.

In a large soup pot, melt the butter and the remaining 2 tablespoons oil over medium-high heat. Add the onion and carrots and sauté until translucent. Add the garlic and thyme leaves and cook for about 1 minute longer. Stir in the cornstarch and Old Bay seasoning. Cook, stirring for 1 minute or until browned (be careful not to let it burn).

Add the broth, then the potatoes and bay leaves. Bring to a boil and cook, uncovered, for about 10 minutes. Add the corn, chicken, and evaporated milk. Stir well, reduce the heat to a simmer, and cook for 5 to 10 minutes until the potatoes are tender. Remove the bay leaves before serving.

+ added yum: Sprinkle each serving with shredded cheddar cheese.

tip

Grill extra corn with a previous meal so this soup can come together even more quickly.

heart of gold soup

ready in 40 minutes

serves 6

4 tablespoons
   unsalted butter

3 leeks, white and light
   green parts, sliced thin

2 cloves garlic, smashed,
   peeled, and chopped

1½ pounds butternut squash,
   peeled and cut into ½-inch
   cubes (about 5 cups)

1½ pounds gold potatoes,
   peeled and cubed
   (about 3 cups)

1 teaspoon kosher salt

½ teaspoon freshly
   ground black pepper

5 to 6 cups chicken broth

1½ cups half-and-half

+ added yum:
   Shredded Gruyère
   cheese and thinly sliced
   chives or scallions

As winter rolls in and chills our bones, we can't say enough about how much we love making a nutritious, warming soup. It's hearty and cozy and the sweetness of leeks and butternut squash make them perfect companions to the hearty earthiness of potatoes. And the gorgeous gold color brings a bright, warm glow to any winter day! Bonus: The soup is loaded with potassium, an electrolyte that helps with muscle contractions and can lower blood pressure in the body.

Melt the butter in a large soup pot or Dutch oven over medium heat. Add the leeks and garlic and sauté for about 2 minutes. (Don't let the garlic burn!) Add the squash, potatoes, salt, and pepper, and sauté for 2 minutes longer.

Add the broth and bring to a boil. Reduce the heat and simmer until the squash and potatoes are very soft, 20 to 25 minutes. Remove the pan from the heat and use an immersion blender to blend the soup until smooth. Blend in the half-and-half and give the soup time to warm through.

+ added yum: Sprinkle each bowl with Gruyère cheese and chives or scallions. Soup time!

 **notes**

quarantine hug soup

ready in 20 minutes
serves 8

⅔ cup extra-virgin olive oil

1 medium sweet yellow
onion, chopped fine

1 leek, white and light green
parts, sliced thin

4 peeled carrots (around 2 cups
baby carrots), chopped

3 stalks celery, chopped

1 fennel bulb, cored
and chopped

A generous handful fresh
parsley, roughly chopped

3 to 4 cloves garlic, smashed,
peeled, and chopped

¼ cup tomato paste

A pinch each of dried oregano,
thyme, and rosemary (a
handful of favorite, fresh
herbs works well too)

8 to 10 cups chicken broth

2 (15-ounce) cans garbanzo
beans, not drained

4 to 5 leaves rainbow
chard, chopped

4 to 5 leaves Tuscan
kale, chopped

2 handfuls baby spinach

Kosher salt and freshly ground
black pepper to taste

+ added yum:
Italian blend cheese and
a squeeze of fresh lemon

This soup was born at the beginning of the covid-19 pandemic when the whole family was back under the same roof and the great no-toilet-paper caper was beginning, the shelves at the grocery stores were cleaned out, and avoiding human contact at the store was stressful. Simply trying to find the items on your list felt more like a scavenger hunt.

With five of us trying to work out of the house, a pot of soup was a great lunch to eat at different times (and eliminate five different messes). We have a couple of go-to healthy vegetable soup recipes we like to make, so we thought we'd whip one up for the week ... but we couldn't find many of the intended ingredients at the store. So we rummaged through the shelves and produce section, and this soup, filled with unexpected substitutes and unexpected deliciousness, was born.

As terrible as the coronavirus time was, it had so much to teach us. We have definitely become more flexible, creative, and patient. There have been so many opportunities for spiritual renewal and growth, and embracing it has brought us comfort. We hope you love this soup as much as we do. It feels especially comforting and meaningful to us because of the way it was created.

Heat the olive oil in a large soup pot over medium-high heat. Add the onions, leek, carrots, celery, fennel, parsley, and garlic, and sauté for about 5 minutes until softened. Add the tomato paste and herbs and stir well.

Add the broth, beans, chard, kale, and spinach, and bring to a simmer. Cook for 5 to 10 minutes on low until the vegetables reach desired texture. Season to taste with salt and pepper.

+ added yum: Finish with cheese and a squeeze of fresh lemon.

tip

This is "kitchen sink" soup; you can throw in any veggies you have or love to use! You can't mess up this soup, you can only adapt it to your own taste.

tuscan kale turkey soup

complete meal

ready in 30 minutes
serves 5 to 6

2 tablespoons extra-virgin
olive oil

1 pound ground turkey

½ pound Italian
sausage meat

1 medium sweet yellow
onion, finely diced

5 cloves garlic, smashed,
peeled, and chopped

6 to 8 cups chicken broth

5 medium gold potatoes,
scrubbed and cut in half
(or one 24-ounce bag
tiny gold potatoes)

8 cups stemmed and
chopped Tuscan kale

1 cup whipping cream

⅔ cup grated Parmesan
cheese

Kosher salt and freshly
ground black
pepper to taste

+ added yum:
More Parmesan cheese
for each bowl

Tuscan kale is the superstar in this cozy and delicious Italian-inspired soup. Tuscan kale—our favorite—is called cavolo nero in Italian, which means "black cabbage," also known as lacinato kale. It has the most beautiful deep forest green color with a cool, dinosaur-skin pattern. You'll see we use it in several of our recipes. It's sweeter and milder in flavor than most kale. We especially love the nutrients it brings! Just one cup provides more than 100 percent of your daily requirements for vitamins A and K, and close to the same for vitamin C!

The Tuscan kale, hints of Italian sausage, and creamy Parmesan broth, lovingly coupled with all of the other honest, hearty, and healthy ingredients, will have you giving yourself lots of praise! Eccellente! Buonissimo! Squisito! Ottimo! Spettacolare!

Heat the oil in a soup pot or Dutch oven over medium-high heat. Add the turkey and sausage and cook, stirring occasionally or until browned. Transfer the meat to a bowl and set aside.

Add the onion to the pot and sauté until soft, 4 to 5 minutes. Add the garlic and cook for 1 minute. Add the broth and bring to a boil. Add the potatoes and simmer until softened, 10 to 13 minutes.

Add the kale and stir well until just softened. Return the meat to the soup and stir in the cream and Parmesan. Simmer for 3 minutes until everything comes together and the soup is warmed through. Season with salt and pepper and serve.

+ added yum: Grate more Parm over each bowl.

 **notes**

white bean chicken chili

complete meal

ready in 45 minutes
serves 4 to 5

3 tablespoons extra-virgin
   olive oil
1 medium yellow onion,
   finely chopped
1 orange bell pepper,
   finely chopped
4 cloves garlic, smashed,
   peeled, and chopped
1½ cups fresh white sweet
   corn or frozen corn
1 (4-ounce) can Hatch green
   chiles, not drained
1 tablespoon chili powder
1 teaspoon ground cumin
1 teaspoon dried oregano
1 teaspoon kosher salt
5 cups chicken broth
1 large rotisserie chicken,
   skin and bones removed,
   meat shredded
2 (15-ounce) cans white
   cannellini beans,
   not drained
Juice of 1 lime
1 package hard, flat tacos/
   tostada shells
+ added yum:
   Shredded Mexican
   blend cheese, sour
   cream, lime wedges,
   chopped fresh cilantro

Some meals get the job done, but they don't really say "fun." If we're eating at home on a weekend night or having friends over, we want to serve something that feels festive and says "cheers to the weekend!" Well, Tex-Mex food of any kind always feels like fun to us. This chili is a great make-ahead and go-have-fun-with-your-people dish. Right before serving time, we heat up a big batch of tostada/hard, flat taco shells for everyone to throw into their bowl. Shredded cheese, sour cream, and a spicy marg … you've got yourself a party!

In a large Dutch oven or soup pot, heat the olive oil over medium heat. Add the onion, bell pepper, and garlic and sauté until the onion is translucent, about 5 minutes (don't let the garlic burn). Add the corn, green chiles, chili powder, cumin, oregano, and salt, stirring well to incorporate. Stir in the broth, chicken, beans, and lime juice. Let simmer on low for 20 to 25 minutes to allow flavors to come together

Follow package instructions for heating and toasting the tostada/flat taco shells.

+ added yum: Serve the chili in bowls with a sprinkling of cheese, dollops of sour cream, squeezes of a fresh lime wedge, and cilantro.

 **notes**

snappy + sassy
salads

Salads inspire all of us to eat more plants and color. And creating salads—full of colors, shapes, and textures—is fun and soulful and brings out the artist in everyone. Throughout the seasons, we find that nature inspires us to incorporate new ingredients into our salads, which elevates them from boring and basic to snappy and sassy. It's a game-changer!

sweet 16 greens salad with you're-a-goddess dressing

ready in 20 minutes
serves however many
you want!

Tuscan kale, chopped
    into bite-size pieces
Baby spinach leaves
Arugula
Swiss chard
Cucumber, cut into rounds
    and quartered
Fresh green beans
Sugar snap peas
Shelled edamame
Romanesco broccoli
Scallions
Zucchini, cut into rounds
    and quartered
Blanched asparagus
Steamed broccolini
Fresh parsley
Pistachios
Pepitas

A salad board is such a fun way to start a dinner party: It's casual, a great conversation starter, and people can serve themselves. Not to mention that it's a sneaky way to skip having to make both apps and a salad. This all-green salad board comprising 16 different greens makes the most gorgeous statement of health and color. You can just feel your body thank you! (You can always pick and choose from this list and use fewer veggies.)

Our creamy and earthy fresh You're-A-Goddess Dressing (next page) also makes a decadent veggie dip, so make extra for your snacks.

You're-a-Goddess Dressing (next page; you may need to double the recipe depending on the number of guests)

Wash and cut the vegetables and greens into various bite-size shapes and arrange by category on your board: Start with mounds of the lettuces, followed by the cucumber, green beans, snap peas, edamame, romanesco, scallions, zuke, asparagus, and broccolini. Finish up with piles of parsley, pistachios and pepitas.

Have a few pairs of easy-to-use tongs by the board and set out pretty bowls for your guests to pile in their custom salad.

tips

- One of the great things about any board is you can use as much or as little of each ingredient as you wish. (You don't have to use 16 different green items.) To figure out the amount of each veggie you want to put on the board, it helps to envision it by assembling one guest bowl or plate and then multiplying that by number of guests. (Of course, we like to add just a bit more to make it a truly grand platter.)
- Clean and prep your veggies earlier in the day so you can be a relaxed hostess for the dinner party

1 (5.3-ounce) container
    vanilla Greek yogurt
    (about ⅔ cup)
1 tablespoon extra-virgin
    olive oil
1 tablespoon fresh
    lemon juice
½ cup fresh basil leaves
½ cup fresh parsley leaves
¼ cup fresh cilantro leaves
6 fresh mint leaves
2 scallions, chopped
1 clove fresh garlic,
    smashed and peeled
Kosher salt and fresh
    ground pepper to taste

you're-a-goddess dressing

Green goddess dressing is one of the first dressings all of the younger Peddies learned to like and probably the main motivation for growing our own herb garden. It's so awesome to be able to just go outside and grab a handful of fresh herbs you have grown, then throw them into a blender to create something beautiful and fresh. We love to make our green goddess dressing lusciously herby and creamy, so it's perfect for any salad and also a wonderful dip companion to fresh veggies!

In a food processor or high-powered blender, combine all the ingredients and pulse until they're mixed well and smooth. Store in an airtight container in the fridge for up to five days.

tip
You can use any combination of herbs you may have on hand.

arugula, fennel + shaved parm salad

plant forward

ready in 20 minutes
serves 6

We definitely did not invent this salad combination, but we really wanted it in our cookbook because it's a salad everyone should have in their repertoire! There are just a few ingredients, but it's perfection when they are married together in the amounts we've tweaked for our taste buds over the years (see Tips). Light, peppery, crunchy, cheesy, lemony, and oh so fresh; everything you want in a salad and a perfect accompaniment to a juicy steak or pork chop!

dressing

3 tablespoons extra-virgin
    olive oil
2 teaspoons fresh lemon juice
½ teaspoon Dijon mustard
1 large clove garlic, peeled
    and grated well
Kosher salt and fresh
    ground pepper to taste

salad

6 heaping cups baby arugula
1 fennel bulb, cored and
    sliced very thin
Zest of 1 small lemon, grated
Shaved Parmesan cheese

 **notes**

make the dressing

In a Mason jar, combine the olive oil, lemon juice, Dijon, garlic, and salt and pepper. Cover and shake well.

assemble the salad

In a large salad bowl or on a platter, lay out the arugula, top with the fennel, and zest the lemon over the top. Shake the dressing, pour over the salad, and toss well. Top with long, slivered shavings of good Parmesan cheese.

tips

- For a sweeter dressing, add 2 teaspoons of honey.
- Make salad dressing ahead if possible. It's not necessary, but the longer the dressing sits, the better the flavors merge. It'll keep for up to one week.

burrata with roasted beets + pistachios

plant forward

**ready in 10 minutes
(with pre-roasted beets)
serves 6**

4 roasted beets (see Roasted
Beets recipe, page 145)
1 (8- to 10-ounce) ball
burrata cheese
Large handful arugula
and/or microgreens
Handful fresh basil, chopped
½ cup roasted pistachios
¼ cup lemon olive
oil (see Tips)
Kosher salt and
pepper to taste

*This salad is visually beautiful with the deep jewel tones of beets
and arugula. The burrata looks so inviting on top, ready to stretch
and spill out with rich delight. It's as delicious as it is gorgeous!*

Arrange the beets in any decorative display on a platter. Place
the burrata in the center of the beets and scatter the greens and
basil over the burrata and beets. Sprinkle the pistachios over the
top and drizzle with lemon olive oil. Season with salt and pepper.

tips

- If you don't have lemon olive oil, serve with a drizzle of regular
  olive oil and a squeeze of fresh lemon for the same kick. Drips
  of fresh pesto are very nice too.
- Any time you roast beets, think of roasting extra so you can
  quickly whip up this special salad!

 **notes**

butter lettuce + castelvetrano olive salad with browned panko

plant forward

ready in 20 minutes
serves 4 to 6

toasted panko

½ cup panko bread crumbs
(gluten-free is OK)
¼ cup freshly grated
Parmesan cheese

dressing

¼ cup extra-virgin olive oil
1 tablespoon Dijon mustard
1 tablespoon fresh
lemon juice
1 tablespoon honey
Kosher salt and
pepper to taste

salad

1 head butter lettuce
1 cup Castelvetrano
olives, kept whole
½ cup roasted pistachios
¼ cup chopped fresh chives
1 cup shaved Parmesan
cheese

One of our favorite things about salad is the endless possibilities of creativity and combinations. When you have the perfect textures and flavors all working together, it's pretty exciting. This simply elegant salad, with just the right amount of crunchy textures and salty flavors, can stand alone as a sophisticated starter. But you can also add a piece of white fish or grilled shrimp for a fine, restaurant-worthy dinner entrée.

toast the panko

Preheat the oven 350°F. Line a baking sheet with parchment paper. In a small bowl, mix the panko and grated Parmesan and spread on the baking sheet. Bake for 2 minutes or until the crumbs are toasted and golden. Stand watch at the oven because this happens fast. Let cool.

make the dressing

In a Mason jar, combine the oil, mustard, lemon juice, and honey. Put on the lid and give a good shake to emulsify. Season to taste with salt and pepper. Shake well again before drizzle time!

assemble the salad

Arrange the butter lettuce, cup sides up, on a large serving platter. Scatter the olives on top, then sprinkle with the pistachios and chives. Drizzle desired amount of dressing all over and distribute the shaved Parm evenly. Sprinkle the toasted panko on top right before serving so it stays crunchy!

 **notes**

peachy quinoa + arugula salad

ready in 20 minutes

serves 4

½ cup hazelnuts, roasted

1 tablespoon extra-virgin
   olive oil, for drizzling

Kosher salt to taste

1 cup quinoa

2 cups water

8 cups arugula

3 ounces goat cheese

3 peaches, pitted
   and sliced thin

Balsamic glaze, for drizzling

 **notes**

How many salads do you know of that meet the requirements of a complete meal? In this gorgeous, colorful salad, you get protein, carbohydrates, veggies, and fat. Warm quinoa, juicy peaches, creamy goat cheese, fresh arugula, and crunchy hazelnuts are a perfect symphony for your taste buds! We love it for lunch, a light dinner, or even a side dish.

Preheat the oven to 350°F. Line a baking sheet with foil.

Place the hazelnuts on the baking sheet, drizzle with about 1 tablespoon olive oil, and toss with a small pinch of salt. Roast until the hazelnuts are browned, about 10 minutes. (Watch closely, they can go from raw to burned quickly.) Remove the hazelnuts from the oven and allow to cool. Transfer to a resealable plastic bag, seal, and gently pound with a mallet or other heavy object to coarsely crush the nuts.

Meanwhile, in a medium saucepan, bring the quinoa and water to a boil. Reduce to a simmer, cover, and cook for 15 minutes or until the grains are translucent and soft.

Arrange the arugula on a platter. Distribute the warm (or room temperature) quinoa over the top and add the goat cheese, peaches, and nuts. Drizzle the balsamic glaze over salad in about 10 lines. Then drizzle olive oil over salad in about 10 lines. Give the salad a quick toss before serving.

persimmon caprese salad

plant forward

ready in 10 minutes
serves 4 to 6

2 ripe persimmons, stemmed
   and very thinly sliced
1 ball mozzarella or
   burrata, thinly sliced
10 leaves fresh basil
3 tablespoons store-
   bought balsamic glaze
2 tablespoons extra-virgin
   olive oil
Salt and freshly ground
   black pepper to taste

We've found that adding more fruit to our grocery baskets adds more interest and nutrition to our meals. So, in walks the persimmon. Talk about interesting! It's becoming very popular because of its sweet, rich, caramel-honey undertones. (When it's perfectly ripe, you can eat it like an apple.) And nutrition? It's high in antioxidants and fiber!

Here we use the persimmon as a fun twist to a traditional caprese salad. Sure, everyone loves a tomato caprese, but if you mix it up a bit, you'll feel so hip and trendy, you'll be making it every persimmon season.

Fun fact: The sweet, seedless variety of the persimmon is also called the Sharon fruit. Look at that, Sharon has her own fruit! It's really named after the Sharon plain in Israel, where it was developed and grows.

Arrange the persimmon slices on a serving platter and top each with a slice of mozzarella, then a basil leaf. Drizzle with balsamic glaze and olive oil and season with salt and pepper to taste.

 **notes**

toasted brussels + pomegranate salad

plant forward

ready in 20 minutes
serves 4 to 5

12 medium Brussels sprouts, halved
3 tablespoons extra-virgin olive oil, divided
Juice of ½ small lime
¼ teaspoon garlic powder
¼ teaspoon onion powder
1 tablespoon balsamic glaze
4 cups fresh baby spinach
2 ounces goat cheese
½ cup pomegranate seeds

 **notes**

This warm gorgeous salad looks like Christmas on a platter and is a treasure box of flavors and textures: the sweet nuttiness of warm roasted Brussels sprouts, the earthiness of goat cheese, the tangy pops of sweet pomegranate seeds. It's a simple but interesting salad, with a sense of style and glam. You can eat it every day or proudly serve it on a special occasion.

Place the Brussels sprouts in a bowl and toss with 1 tablespoon of the olive oil, the lime juice, garlic powder, and onion powder.

Heat another 1 tablespoon of the olive oil in a skillet over medium heat. Lay the Brussels, cut side down, in the hot pan and cook undisturbed until browned on the bottom, about 5 minutes. Flip each one over and cook for another 5 to 7 minutes until browned all over and the centers are tender. (Large sprouts will require an additional minute or two on each side.)

Meanwhile, in a separate small bowl, combine the balsamic glaze and the remaining 1 tablespoon olive oil.

To assemble the salad, arrange the baby spinach on a platter. Top with Brussels sprouts, goat cheese, and pomegranate seeds. Drizzle the balsamic–olive oil dressing over all and serve. No need to toss unless you'd like to.

tips

- The salad also works well with oven-roasted Brussels: Roast the seasoned Brussels sprout halves on a baking sheet at 400°F (flipping them halfway through) for 20 to 25 minutes or until desired level of crispiness.
- The dressing is a matter of taste: Use whatever ratio of olive oil and balsamic glaze you like. We like a 1:1 ratio, but go ahead and add more olive oil for a richer dressing, or more balsamic glaze for a sweeter, tangier dressing.

tuscan kale + blueberry + grilled corn salad

plant forward

20 minutes

serves 4 (but easy to
scale up or down)

2 ears corn, grilled
3 cups torn Tuscan kale
3 cups torn rainbow chard
2 cups blueberries
1 cup roasted pecans
1 cup goat cheese

warm maple dijon dressing

1 cup extra-virgin olive oil
3 garlic cloves, grated
½ cup maple syrup
¼ cup balsamic vinegar
¼ cup Dijon mustard
Kosher salt and freshly
    ground black
    pepper to taste

 **notes**

We all love grilled corn—a lot—so we always make sure to throw a few extra cobs on the grill to use in soups and, especially, this salad, which we've made for years. There's something so satisfying about biting into fresh-off-the-cob corn, with chunks of the kernels still intact. The warm dressing is also key as it slightly melts the goat cheese and marries all of the ingredients together. It's so rich and satisfying as just a salad, but it's also the perfect partner for anything off the grill!

for the salad

Use a sharp knife to cut the kernels from the corn cobs, keeping some together in chunks. Transfer to a serving bowl and add the remaining salad ingredients.

for the dressing

Heat the oil in a medium saucepan over medium heat. Add the garlic and sauté for a minute, then whisk in the maple syrup, vinegar, and mustard. Bring to a boil and stir for 1 minute or until the ingredients are combined and the dressing is warm. Remove from heat.

Toss the salad with your desired amount of warm dressing, add salt and pepper to taste, and it's ready to serve! You can store any leftover salad dressing in the fridge in a sealed container for up to five days.

tip

We've varied the way we serve this recipe over the years. It's good with all different greens, but the key is to have a warm ingredient to melt the goat cheese. So instead of a warm dressing, serve it at room temp, but then shave kernels of hot-off-the-grill corn directly onto the salad.

apps + snacks

We hate to brag, but we are really good at snacking! Snack time in kindergarten was everything and, let's face it, none of us ever really grow out of snack-time excitement. Whether it's social time with friends or quiet time alone, a snack break is refreshing and provides us with energy to continue our day.

And when it comes to appetizers, we like think of them as a happy hostess who opens the door and greets guests with fun music bumpin', a warm smile, and a giant hug. That is, appetizers should set the tone for a fun evening.

medjool dates + goat cheese + crushed pistachios

ready in 15 minutes
serves 6 to 12

12 Medjool dates
2 ounces soft goat cheese,
    room temperature
1 teaspoon honey, plus
    more for drizzling
¼ teaspoon turmeric
¼ teaspoon black pepper,
    plus more for garnish
1½ tablespoons pistachio
    nuts, crushed

 **notes**

We all need at least one special and swanky appetizer we can whip up in 15 minutes or less. This recipe makes dates easy and approachable. The unique flavors and textures come together in a beautiful and incredibly satisfying boat of decadence. We think you're going to bring these cute dates on a lot of dates—but no one's going to let you take them home!

Using a sharp paring knife, make a lengthwise slit in the middle of each date but don't cut all the way through; you are just creating a well to remove the pit and then add the filling.

Mix the goat cheese, honey, turmeric, and pepper. Fill the open dates with the mixture, about 1 teaspoon per date. Sprinkle each filled date with pistachios and give a nice twist of freshly ground black pepper over each one. Drizzle the serving plate with honey.

crispy crab cakes with quick caper sauce

tradition
♥

ready in 1 hour, 40 minutes
(includes 1 hour to chill)
makes 8

1 tablespoon vegetable oil,
    plus more for the pan
½ cup chopped red bell pepper
3 scallions (green and white
    parts), chopped
3 cloves garlic, smashed,
    peeled, and finely chopped
1 egg, beaten
2 tablespoons
    Worcestershire sauce
1 tablespoon Dijon mustard
Pinch kosher salt
2 twists/grinds freshly
    ground black pepper
1 pound fresh crab meat chunks
2 cups panko crumbs,
    divided (gluten-free
    panko works great too)
¼ cup grated Parmesan cheese
2 teaspoons Old Bay seasoning
2 tablespoons chopped
    fresh parsley
Grated zest and juice
    1 small lemon, plus lemon
    wedges for serving
2 tablespoons unsalted butter

quick caper sauce

1 cup sour cream
2 tablespoons capers, plus
    1 tablespoon caper juice
1 tablespoon chopped
    fresh chives
Grated zest and juice
    of ½ small lemon
⅛ teaspoon garlic powder
Kosher salt and fresh ground
    pepper to taste

Over the years, we've figured out that sometimes it's nice to stay home on New Year's Eve. The hustle and bustle of the holiday season can be exhausting, and by the time we get to NYE, we just want to stay home. But still, we do want to bring in the new year with a little pomp and circumstance, so we make a special meal at home. Rather than waiting until midnight, we crack open the champagne and start NYE with this scrumptious crab cake appetizer. It's glitz and glamour in your jammies and a relaxed, festive way to ring in the new year!

Heat the oil in medium skillet over medium heat. Add the red pepper, scallions, and garlic and sauté for 3 minutes or until the vegetables are slightly softened. Set aside to cool.

In a small bowl, whisk together the egg, Worcestershire, mustard, salt, and pepper. In a large bowl, stir together the crab, 1 cup panko, Parmesan, Old Bay, parsley, and lemon zest and juice. Fold in the cooled veggies and egg mixture.

♡ notes

Form the crab mixture into eight patties. Sprinkle the remaining 1 cup panko on a plate. Dredge each patty in the crumbs to coat on both sides. Transfer to a plate, cover, and refrigerate for 1 hour to soften the panko and bind the mixture for frying.

Coat the bottom of a large skillet with oil. Over medium heat, add the butter, and once it and the oil start doing a shimmery dance, add the crab cakes and cook for 4 to 5 minutes on each side until golden brown.

make the caper sauce

Combine all the ingredients and stir well.

Serve the warm crab cakes with lemon wedges and caper sauce.

herby roasted cauliflower

plant forward

ready in 1 hour
serves 6

1 large head cauliflower
⅓ cup extra-virgin olive oil
½ cup grated Parmesan
   cheese
1 teaspoon ground cumin
1 teaspoon chili powder
1 teaspoon paprika
1 teaspoon garlic powder
1 teaspoon dried basil
1 teaspoon dried thyme
1 teaspoon dried parsley
½ teaspoon onion powder
½ teaspoon ground turmeric
½ teaspoon kosher or sea salt
¼ teaspoon black pepper

 **notes**

This savory, roasted cauliflower appetizer will inspire you to skip the cheese and crackers and think of a roasted veggie starter more often. Not only is it quite impressive looking as it arrives on the serving board, it's yummilicious and nutritious!

Rinse the cauliflower head and trim the stem, being careful not to cut off too much so the head stays intact. Place the cauliflower in a large bowl and cover with plastic wrap. Microwave for 5 minutes or until it softens slightly. (It shouldn't still be rock hard, but we don't want it to be too soft and falling apart). Remove from the bowl and pat dry. Set on a baking sheet lined with foil and let sit for at least 15 minutes.

Preheat the oven to 400°F.

In a mixing bowl, whisk together the oil, Parmesan, and all the seasonings. Brush the mixture all over the cauliflower.

Bake the cauliflower on a center rack for 30 minutes or until golden, crispy brown, and tender. Serve on a platter with a sharp knife and forks for each person. You can cut up the cauliflower at the table, or each guest can cut off their desired piece.

tips

- After microwaving the cauliflower, be careful of the steam as you remove the plastic wrap.
- Make sure the cauliflower is dry before beginning the coating and baking process.

street corn dip

ready in 15 minutes

serves 8

8 ounces cream cheese

½ cup sour cream

1½ teaspoons ground cumin

1 teaspoon chili powder

Juice of ½ lime

2 tablespoons
  unsalted butter

3 cups fresh or thawed
  frozen corn kernels

¼ cup chopped fresh cilantro

3 scallions (white & green
  parts), sliced thin

½ cup cotija cheese

Corn chips for serving

+ added yum:
  Paprika and
  additional cilantro

 **notes**

This is one of those apps that's the first to disappear at any party or gathering. Some friends ask us to bring it along every single time we visit. It's taken many forms over the years—sometimes served hot, sometimes cold, sometimes we substituted Greek yogurt for the cream cheese when we served it cold. It brings all the fun of elote (Mexican street corn), customized to your personal preferences. It is savory, sweet, salty, and definitely a crowd-pleaser.

Combine the cream cheese, sour cream, cumin, chili powder, and lime juice in a large mixing bowl.

In a large skillet, melt the butter over medium heat. Add the corn and sauté for 3 to 5 minutes until warmed through. Remove from heat and allow to cool slightly.

Add the cream cheese mixture to the corn and combine well. Add the cilantro, scallions, and cotija cheese and mix well. Pour the dip into a serving dish. Serve with your favorite corn chips. We love blue corn chips.

+ added yum: Sprinkle the top with paprika and additional fresh cilantro.

tip

You can also add a bit of chili powder to give this dish a nice kick.

silky fava bean dip

ready in 10 minutes

serves 10

1 (14-ounce) can fava
    beans, drained
¼ cup lemon olive oil
3 cloves fresh garlic,
    smashed, peeled,
    and chopped
Juice of 1 small lemon
½ teaspoon champagne
    vinegar
Kosher salt to taste
Fresh veggies and/or
    Your Kitchen's Warm,
    Fresh Pita Bread
    (page 112) for serving
+ added yum:
    Lemon olive oil, pistachio
    nuts, paprika

 **notes**

We have a tradition in our family that when a daughter graduates from college, she gets to choose a destination for a mother/daughter trip. Kendall chose Greece. We were inspired by all of the delicious dips they make from various beans and peas on their islands. One of our favorites was the dip called "fava."

During quarantine, we wanted to make our own fava, so we ordered some fava beans online. True confession: Only after we ordered the beans did we start our research—and we found that Greek fava isn't actually made from fava beans but yellow split peas. Since we were now proud owners of a small case of canned fava beans, we made our own version. The decadent, fiber- and protein-rich dip is silky and tastes so close to the dips we remembered in Greece that we decided to keep this recipe. It just goes to show us that some of the best recipes come from mistakes.

Combine the fava beans, lemon oil, garlic, lemon juice, vinegar, and salt in a food processor or a nutribullet and pulse until well combined and silky.

Serve with fresh veggies and pita bread, topping the dip with **+ added yum** garnishes of choice.

mezze board inspo

 **notes**

A Greek mezze is a selection of small dishes served as appetizers. Grazing a board full of fun and interesting small plates is one of our absolute, favorite ways to eat! We believe there's no right or wrong way to build a mezze board. To create this one, we combined some of our favorite apps and snacks: Greek Islands Tzatziki (page 111); Your Kitchen's Warm, Fresh Pita Bread (page 112); Did Someone Say Falafel? (page 115); Silky Fava Bean Dip (page 107); plus fresh veggies and assorted cheeses.

greek islands tzatziki

ready in 20 minutes
serves 8

2 cups grated cucumber
(about 2 medium
cucumbers)

2 tablespoons chopped
fresh mint

1½ cups plain vanilla
Greek yogurt

1 tablespoon extra-virgin
olive oil

1 tablespoon fresh
lemon juice

1 clove fresh garlic, smashed,
peeled, and minced

½ teaspoon sea salt
(if you're using "pinches,"
pay attention to how
many fingers you are
using as to not oversalt)

A favorite snack Sharon and Kendall fell in love with over the warm summer days in Greece was classic tzatziki, a tasty and refreshing, yogurty dip that has both bright and mellow flavors.

Sharon and Kendall learned to make it in a cooking class given by a beautiful lady named Teta in Mykonos. They learned so much that day about Mykonian lifestyle and made so many different things ... but don't remember the exact recipe 100 percent. Nonetheless, this is delicious, we promise!

It is truly refreshing and a perfect dip for fresh veggies, Your Kitchen's Warm, Fresh Pita Bread (page 112), and Did Someone Say Falafel? (page 115). It also makes a great accompaniment for meat or fish.

Place the grated cucumber in a light, clean, thin dish towel and twist and squeeze over the sink to wring out excess water. Take your time with this step. You may have to wring the cucumber a couple of times.

In a large bowl, combine the cucumber, mint, yogurt, olive oil, lemon juice, and garlic and thoroughly combine. Season with salt and serve.

Fun fact: Sharon and Kendall won Teta's tzatziki contest. Really! They credited it to remembering Teta's wonderful tips: Avoid oversalting by paying attention to how many fingers you use in a "pinch" (too many can make the tzatziki too salty and you can't turn back), and be patient when wringing water out of the cucumber to avoid watery tzatziki.

Kendall and Sharon at a Mykonian farm cooking class in Mykonos, Greece

your kitchen's warm, fresh pita bread

ready in 2 hours

serves 8

1 cup warm water
(105°F to 110°F)

1 (¼-ounce) package
(2¼ teaspoons)
active dry yeast

1 teaspoon sugar

Up to 3½ cups all-purpose
flour, divided, plus more
for kneading if needed

1½ tablespoons extra-virgin
olive oil, plus more for
the bowl and skillet

1 teaspoon kosher salt

 **notes**

During quarantine, we got into making different types of bread. Pita with hummus has always been one of our favorite snacks, so we gave pita bread a try. Like all bread, it takes several steps and a little patience, but this recipe is totally doable and produces pita bread that is the perfect chewy, crunchy texture! We suggest making any dips (like Silky Fava Bean Dip, page 107, and Greek Islands Tzatziki, page 111) ahead of time so you can immediately dip in as soon as the warm pitas come off the skillet.

Combine the warm water, yeast, and sugar in the bowl of a stand mixer. Stir with fork until completely dissolved. With the whisk paddle attached, turn the mixer on low and slowly add ½ cup flour until combined well. Let rest for 15 minutes or until the mixture starts to foam and look like a sponge. Add the oil, salt, and 2 cups flour. Mix well with paddle attachment until the mixture forms a sticky, shaggy dough.

Attach the dough hook to the mixer, sprinkle a little flour over the dough, and knead for 5 minutes on low or until it's a smooth dough ball. If the dough feels overly sticky at any point, add more flour in small increments but be careful not to add too much; the dough should be soft and moist. Grease a large glass bowl with olive oil. Drop the dough ball into a bowl and cover with plastic wrap. Place in a warm place and allow to proof until it has doubled in size, about 1 hour. (After proofing, you can store the dough in the refrigerator for up to 24 hours, or begin to prepare it to cook immediately. If stored in the refrigerator, let it sit on the counter for 20 to 30 minutes—the dough should warm up perfectly from there through rolling and shaping.)

Pat down the dough and divide into eight even-sized balls. Let the dough balls rest for at least 10 minutes after shaping.

Lightly flour a surface for rolling. Take one dough ball and roll into a ¼-inch-thick disc that is about 8 inches in diameter. Brush a cast iron skillet with 1 teaspoon olive oil and heat over medium heat until a drop of water sizzles. Add the dough round and let the pita cook, turning once or until you start to see air pockets form and the bread starts to appear toasted brown, about 2 minutes per side.

Repeat, rolling out and cooking all eight dough balls, stacking the cooked pitas on a plate with a piece of foil or kitchen towel on top to keep them warm. Use a pizza cutter or sharp knife to cut pitas in triangles if desired.

did someone say falafel?

plant forward

ready in 1 hour
makes about 20

1½ yellow onions,
    coarsely chopped
3 garlic cloves, smashed
    and chopped
1 cup chopped fresh cilantro
1 cup chopped fresh parsley
2 (15-ounce) cans
    chickpeas, drained
½ cup chickpea flour
1½ teaspoons baking powder
1½ teaspoons ground
    cardamom
1½ teaspoons ground cumin
1½ teaspoons kosher salt
1 teaspoon freshly ground
    black pepper
Vegetable oil for frying

 **notes**

What the heck is falafel, right? Well, if you're new to it, it is delicious, crispy, deep-fried fritter balls made of herby, mashed chickpeas. Think hush puppy texture. It's a favorite, fast-casual dish and street food staple in Middle Eastern countries, naturally vegetarian, and high in protein and fiber. It is also really fun to say: Go ahead, say it three times fast. Falafel, falafel, falafel! Falafel is often served in wraps, pitas, and salads and accompanied by hummus and tahini sauce.

In a food processor, pulse the onions, garlic, cilantro, and parsley until everything is chopped and blended. Add the chickpeas, chickpea flour, baking powder, cardamom, cumin, salt, and pepper. Blend until well combined. Form the mixture into about 20 balls, each about the size of a ping-pong ball.

In a Dutch oven or large pot, heat at least 3 inches of oil to 350°F. Using a spider spatula, lower about 5 falafel balls into the hot oil without crowding the pan. Fry until crispy and golden brown, about 5 minutes. (Doing small batches of 5 will keep the grease hot and cooking process quicker.) Transfer to a baking sheet lined with paper towels to soak up excess oil. Repeat with the remaining balls. Serve right away.

real-deal triple truffle popcorn

ready in 10 minutes
makes 10 cups

3 tablespoons vegetable oil
½ cup popcorn kernels
   (see Tips)
4 ounces truffle
   Gouda cheese
3 to 4 drizzles of truffle oil
Truffle salt to taste

 **notes**

Beware, the three layers of truffle flavor in this indulgent popcorn make this very addicting! And it's a perfect, quick, bougie snack to catch up with a friend over a delicious glass of wine, maybe an Oregon Pinot Noir. There is so much of life's magnificent romance in simple elegance and perfect pairings.

Line a large tray with parchment paper.

In a very large pot, combine the oil and popcorn, cover, and place over medium heat. Cook, occasionally lifting and shaking the pot until most all of the kernels have popped.

Dump the popcorn evenly onto the parchment-lined tray. Immediately grate the truffle cheese all over the popcorn while it's hot. Drizzle with the truffle oil and sprinkle on a bit of truffle salt—a little at a time of both, tasting after each addition. Toss well with your hands and serve.

tips

- We use Orville Redenbacher kernel (stovetop) popcorn here. Follow instructions on the package if you use a different brand.
- There is such a superior difference in the flavor and texture of popcorn when it's popped in good oil on the stove versus a microwave bag, but in a pinch, you can toss microwave popcorn with the cheese, oil, and salt for a quicker version.
- Use a large pot—at least 8 quarts—to pop the popcorn.
- Sprinkling a fresh herb onto popped corn is fun too!

"the cheeseball"

tradition

ready in 15 minutes

serves 8

2 (8-ounce) blocks cream
cheese, room temperature

1 (8-ounce) bag shredded
medium or sharp
cheddar cheese

1 (4- or 5-ounce) container
blue cheese, divided

1 (8-ounce) can crushed
pineapple, drained
very well

3 scallions (white and green
parts), sliced thin

Worcestershire sauce to taste

Kosher salt and freshly
ground black
pepper to taste

1 (8-ounce) bag pecans,
chopped

♡ notes

Every time we even mention "the cheeseball," I'm pretty sure you can hear music. It is a legend among family and friends. You know something beautiful is about to be celebrated whenever the cheeseball is mentioned. Thanksgiving, Christmas, birthdays, weddings, Fourth of July—this ball of goodness makes any special occasion that much more special!

In a large mixing bowl or stand mixer, combine the cream cheese, cheddar cheese, and two-thirds of the container of blue cheese. (You may want to add all of blue cheese after tasting, but start slow.) Add the well-drained pineapple, scallions, and Worcestershire to taste. (We generally start by adding 6 to 8 heavy shakes.) Add a pinch of salt and pepper and mix everything together. We recommend giving it a taste now. Some people like it with more or less blue cheese or Worcestershire sauce, but we can't get enough Worcestershire.

On a cutting board, spread out the pecan pieces. Use your hands (remove your rings!) to form your giant ball of cheese. Drop it onto the pecans and roll it around until the whole ball is covered in nuts. Wrap in wax, parchment paper, or plastic wrap and refrigerate until ready for serving, up to three days. Serve with your favorite crackers.

tip

Be sure to drain the pineapple well or the cheese won't form into a firm ball.

warm-spiced roasted chickie peas

plant forward

ready in 20 minutes
serves 8

1 (15.5-ounce) can chickpeas (a.k.a. garbanzo beans), drained well

2 tablespoons extra-virgin olive oil

1 teaspoon ground turmeric

1 teaspoon ground cumin

½ teaspoon garlic powder

½ teaspoon onion powder

½ teaspoon thyme leaves

 **notes**

It's so fun to get a spontaneous invitation to join friends for a little happy hour, but showing up empty-handed is not something we like to do. That's why we keep our pantries stocked with chickpeas and a variety of spices, making it easy to create a delicious, plant-based, protein-packed snack on a whim. And you can have fun developing your own different seasonings for this oh-so-easy snack. We also offer a variation to get you started.

Preheat the oven to 400°F. Line a large baking sheet with parchment paper or foil.

Pour the chickpeas into a medium mixing bowl and pat them well to dry. Add the olive oil and all the seasonings and toss to coat chickpeas evenly.

Spread the chickpeas on the baking sheet in a single layer. Roast for 15 to 20 minutes, then roll them around to prevent burning. Roast for an additional 15 to 20 minutes or until desired crispiness. We like them crispy with a tad of their original texture—not too hard to the bite.

variation

roasted chickie peas with parmesan + rosemary

Swap out the spice mix for ¼ cup grated Parmesan cheese, 1 teaspoon dried rosemary, 1 teaspoon garlic powder, and ½ teaspoon onion powder. Season with salt to taste after roasting.

tips

- Every oven is different, so be sure to check the chickpeas after the first 20 minutes so they don't burn.
- This can be done in an air fryer at 375°F for 10 to 15 minutes.
- You can buy cute little scoops on Amazon for serving. It prevents a lot of fingers in the bowl!

say cheeeeese fondue

tradition

ready in 20 minutes

serves 4 to 5

1 pound good Gruyère
    cheese, shredded

2 tablespoons cornstarch

1 cup white wine of choice

1 tablespoon fresh
    lemon juice

2 cloves garlic, peeled
    and halved

½ teaspoon dry mustard

⅛ teaspoon nutmeg

 **notes**

Our family's Christmas Eve fondue kicks off the Christmas festivities in just the right way! After coming home from evening mass, we turn on some Christmas carols, open up a nice bottle of wine, bring out the fondue pot, and huddle around it like it's a cozy fire. We load up a large board with all sorts of fruit, veggie, and bread dippers, then watch the cheese slowly melt—it builds the excitement, like waiting for Santa! Of course, a fondue party is always in season, so don't be shy about pulling out your fondue pot all year long.

Favorite dippers of all sorts: bite-size cubes of baguette, asparagus, broccoli, cauliflower, carrot sticks, sliced pears, sliced apples, etc.

Prepare your board with assorted dippers. Leave space in the middle for your fondue pot.

In a resealable bag, combine the cheese and cornstarch and shake to lightly coat the cheese shreds. This prevents the cornstarch from flying around the kitchen and saves you from another dirty dish!

Warm the wine, lemon juice, and garlic in your fondue pot over medium heat. Let gently simmer for a few minutes, allowing the garlic to infuse. (You can remove garlic after this stage, or leave it for garlic lovers.) Gradually add the cheese, stirring constantly or until it's all in and smooth. Add the mustard and nutmeg, stirring well.

You're ready for dipping and fondue fun!

tips

- Add the cheese *gradually* to ensure a smooth, not clumpy, fondue.
- You can blanch the vegetables or serve them raw. We serve them raw and in small-bite sizes.
- Try to keep your fondue pot at a medium temperature to make dippers easily edible and prevent burning on the bottom of the pot.

pan-seared scallops with baked apples + citrus

ready in 40 minutes
serves 8

3 Honeycrisp apples, peeled,
cored, and sliced into
⅓-inch-thick discs

4 tablespoons
unsalted butter

¼ cup packed raw
brown sugar

1 to 2 teaspoons
ground cinnamon

8 pan-seared scallops
(see Greece-Inspired
Buttery Pan-Seared
Scallops with Pea Puree
recipe, page 218)

1 orange, peeled and
sliced into thin discs

1 blood orange, peeled and
sliced into thin discs

1 (1.75-ounce) package
of microgreens

 **notes**

This sophisticated starter was inspired by the mother-daughter trip to Greece after Kendall graduated from college. We tried to recreate the mezze, or small plate, we had in a charming restaurant called M-eating in Mykonos. Their dishes were so clever and fresh. The combination of buttery, seared scallops on top of baked apples with fresh citrus was one of the tastiest combinations we've ever had.

Preheat the oven to 350°F. Coat a 9 by 13-inch casserole dish with a thin layer of cooking spray, then arrange the apple discs in it in an even layer. Melt the butter in a small saucepan over medium heat, add the sugar and cinnamon, and stir well. Pour the mixture all over the apple discs. Bake for 20 minutes or until the apples are soft but not mushy.

Spread out the baked apple discs on a platter and arrange the seared scallops on top. Place orange slices between each apple and scallop stack. Sprinkle generously with microgreens and serve warm.

tip

We like Honeycrisp apples, but you can use Pink Lady, Granny Smith, or Jonagold. All bake deliciously and hold their shape well.

sunny mango salsa

ready in 20 minutes

serves 8

2 mangos, peeled and diced

3 Roma tomatoes, diced

½ small shallot, diced

½ jalapeño chile,
    seeded and diced

¼ cup chopped fresh cilantro

3 tablespoons lime juice

1 teaspoon apple
    cider vinegar

⅛ teaspoon black pepper

⅛ teaspoon garlic powder

Some dishes just taste like vacation, and the bright flavors of this mango salsa immediately bring visions of turquoise waters and orange-lit sunsets. We love scoops and scoops of the fruity, nontraditional salsa on corn chips for a flirty snack. It's also perfect for garnishing a piece of fresh fish or stuffing into fish tacos. (Or any kind of tacos!)

Combine the mangos, tomatoes, shallot, and jalapeño in a large bowl. Add the cilantro, lime juice, and vinegar, then stir to coat the ingredients well. Season with pepper and garlic powder and stir gently. You're ready to serve your sunshine in a bowl!

 **notes**

spring harvest board inspo

We hope our cookbook will inspire you to build lots of different kinds of boards. It's such a great way to exercise your creativity— with the bonus of providing friends and family a fun way to gather and graze.

As we said, there is no right way or wrong way to build a board, so don't let anything you read intimidate you into thinking there are "rules" you have to follow. The beauty of a board is in the person who creates it. No two boards will be the same, and that's why we love them.

Challenge yourself every season to see what looks fresh and delicious and build a board of colors, health, and fun! We created this board for Easter brunch, but it could also be used to hold everyone over until a meal, as a brunch with friends— whatever we want!

If you're not sure where to start with your board, we suggest a little of everything: good bread, some meats, cheeses, and fresh veggies, then add fresh and/or dried fruits, nuts, seeds, spreads, jams, and dips!

artsy focaccia bread

ready in 12+ hours
    (includes resting dough)
serves 10

1 (¼-ounce) package
    (2¼ teaspoons)
    active dry yeast
⅛ teaspoon sugar
3 cups warm water
    (105°F to 110°F), divided
6¼ cups bread flour
1 tablespoon kosher salt
1 tablespoon finely chopped
    fresh rosemary
5 tablespoons extra-virgin
    olive oil, divided
Vegetables and herbs
    for decorating:
sliced peppers of all colors,
    olives, sliced tomatoes,
    capers, herbs like
    rosemary or parsley—or
    any other veggie favorites
Flaky finishing sea salt

 **notes**

During the covid-19 pandemic when we all had more time on our hands, many were inspired by Instagram and TikTok foodies to make all kinds of breads. Since we love focaccia and being creative, we decided to give artsy bread a try! Depending on what you have in your produce drawer or herb garden, the artistic possibilities are endless. The bread canvas is all yours to create a masterpiece.

In a small bowl, combine the yeast, sugar, and ½ cup of warm water. Stir until the yeast and sugar are dissolved. Let rest until the mixture becomes foamy, about 5 minutes.

Using a stand mixer with a hook attachment, combine the flour with the remaining 2½ cups warm water. Mix slowly on low speed, stopping occasionally to scrape flour from the sides to incorporate it until a rough dough ball starts to form. Pour in the yeast mixture and mix on low speed again until the dough absorbs all the additional liquid, about a minute. Add the salt and rosemary and continue mixing on medium speed until it's fully incorporated and the dough looks elastic. It will be sticky!

Pour 3 tablespoons of the oil into a large glass bowl and swirl it around to coat the whole bowl. Scrape the dough into the bowl with a large plastic spatula and turn to coat with oil. Cover and put in a warm place to proof for 2 to 3 hours or until the dough has doubled in size. Place a piece of tape on the outside of the bowl to mark where the dough starts so you can see how much it rises.

Grease the bottom and rims of an 18 x 13-inch rimmed baking sheet with the remaining 2 tablespoons oil.

Fold the dough inside the bowl a few times to deflate it, then drop onto the prepared baking sheet. Using well-oiled hands, lift up the dough and fold it over a few times. Cover the dough with plastic wrap (making sure the dough has enough oil on top to prevent sticking). Let rest for 10 minutes.

Being careful not to tear the dough, stretch it wide then long into a rectangle that reaches all four sides of the baking sheet. If dough starts to spring away from the sides, let it sit for a few minutes and try again. Immediately cover the dough again with the oiled plastic. Refrigerate for 8 to 24 hours.

Take the dough out of the refrigerator and set in a warm place for about 45 minutes so it can rise and puff up to the top of the baking sheet. (While you're waiting, begin prepping the veggies and herbs for your masterpiece. Try laying out ideas on a cutting board before applying to bread.)

Preheat the oven to 450°F. Make sure your rack is exactly in the middle for even baking.

When the dough has risen and you're ready to get artsy, remove the plastic wrap and drizzle the focaccia with oil. Apply your design and drizzle with more oil. Bake for 25 minutes or until desired golden color. Immediately after removing the focaccia from the oven, sprinkle generously with flaky finishing sea salt. Let it cool before lifting to a cutting board with spatulas and cutting into squares to serve.

we'll be by
your sides

We feel the characteristics of a good side should be much like that of a good friend and sidekick: supportive, dependable, and not too high maintenance. And just like our friends, we want our sides to be good contributors to the nutrients in our life, but sometimes, it's OK for them to just provide some fun!

creamy coconut lentils + veggie friends

plant
forward

ready in 40 minutes

serves 4 to 6

2 tablespoons extra-virgin
    olive oil, plus more
    for drizzling

2 tablespoons
    unsalted butter

3 carrots, peeled
    and chopped

2 stalks celery, chopped

1 small sweet yellow
    onion, chopped

4 cloves fresh garlic,
    smashed, peeled,
    and chopped

2 tablespoons chopped
    fresh parsley

2 teaspoons fresh
    thyme leaves

1 teaspoon ground turmeric

½ teaspoon fresh ground
    black pepper

4 cups chicken broth

2 cups brown lentils

2 medium sweet potatoes,
    peeled and chopped

1 bay leaf

1 (14.5-ounce) can
    coconut milk

3 cups fresh baby spinach

Let's get some lentils in your life! Lentils are part of the legume family but don't require any presoaking and are ready pretty quickly. They're not only nutritious (high in protein, iron, and potassium) but sooooo scrumptious and add delicious heartiness to many dishes. These creamy, coconutty lentils are a comforting, lively super side but can also stand on their own, especially for weekday lunches.

In a large stockpot or Dutch oven, heat the oil and butter over medium-high heat. Add the carrots, celery, and onion, and sauté until softened, about 5 minutes. Add the garlic, parsley, thyme, turmeric, and pepper and sauté for 1 to 2 minutes. Add the broth, lentils, sweet potatoes, and bay leaf. Simmer for 30 minutes or until the lentils and potatoes are tender and most of the liquid is gone.

Stir in the coconut milk and blend well. Stir in the spinach and let simmer until the spinach is wilted and the coconut milk is warm—this happens quickly, just 1 to 2 minutes. Remove the bay leaf and discard. Serve the lentils with a drizzle of olive oil.

 **notes**

root vegetable gratin

ready in 1 hour, 30 minutes
serves 8 to 10

3 tablespoons unsalted
  butter, softened
2 medium red beets
2 medium yellow beets
2 to 3 medium golden
  potatoes
1 to 2 long, thin sweet
  potatoes
2 parsnips
2 cups heavy cream
5 ounces Parmesan
  cheese, grated, plus
  more for topping
Leaves from 10 sprigs
  fresh thyme
3 cloves fresh garlic, grated
Kosher salt and ground
  black pepper
1 cup shredded
  Gruyère cheese

We believe everyone should perfect a dish that they can bring to a gathering that gets all of the ooooohs and ahhhhhhs. This one is both divine and—thanks to our stacking technique—totally Pinterest-worthy. Using a mandolin or thinly slicing all of the colorful veggies is wonderfully therapeutic. Not only is this a sneaky way to introduce root vegetables to all ages, it's just absolutely gorgeous and empowering to make.

Preheat the oven 350°F. Grease a 9 x 13-inch baking dish with the softened butter.

Peel and very thinly slice the red beets, yellow beets, potatoes, sweet potatoes, and parsnips, placing each vegetable in their own medium bowl. Combine the cream, Parmesan, and thyme leaves in a separate bowl, then equally divide the mixture among the five bowls of vegetables. Toss the vegetables to evenly coat.

Scatter the garlic on the bottom of the greased baking dish. With your hands, place each vegetable in the dish, standing them up in the dish and arranging in rows. (Hint: Start lining them up from the outside in and begin with the smallest on the outside. Or choose any design you wish!)

When the vegetables are all nestled in, pour any leftover cream from the veggie bowls into the baking dish, but not the cream from the red beets as it will turn everything pink. Sprinkle with salt and pepper to taste, then more Parmesan.

Cover with foil and bake until the veggies are soft. Baking time varies; we suggest beginning to check after 50 to 55 minutes, but they could take slightly more than an hour. Remove the foil and sprinkle generously with the Gruyère. Continue baking until the veggies are tender to the touch and the cheese is golden and bubbly, 2 to 3 minutes.

tips

- Adjust the number of vegetables to the size of the baking dish. Lay the whole vegetables in the dish to get an idea of how much to slice up.
- You can use more or less Parmesan cheese.

 **notes**

cannellini bean puree with candied parsnips + crispy lentils

plant forward

**ready in 1 hour
serves 4 to 5**

crispy lentils

1½ cups lentils, rinsed

4 cups chicken or
vegetable broth

6 sprigs fresh thyme

4 teaspoons extra-virgin
olive oil

1 teaspoon garlic powder

candied parsnips

4 parsnips, peeled and
sliced in half (or
quartered, if larger)

2 tablespoons maple syrup

2 tablespoons olive oil

2 tablespoons brown sugar

cannellini puree

2 tablespoons lemon olive
oil, plus more for drizzling

1 small shallot, chopped

4 cloves fresh garlic,
smashed, peeled,
and chopped

2 (15-ounce) cans cannellini
beans, drained

Grated zest and juice
of 1 small lemon

Kosher salt

Bean purees—trendy dishes we are seeing more and more on restaurant menus, Pinterest, and Instagram—not only look pretty, but are downright delicious. They're also a great way to add more protein to our diet. Our silky and smooth cannellini puree is topped with candied parsnips and crispy lentils for a supporting dish that can also be the leading lady on a meatless Monday.

Preheat the oven to 350°F. Line two baking sheets with parchment paper.

prep the crispy lentils

Combine the lentils, broth, and thyme in a medium saucepan and bring to a boil. Reduce the heat and simmer until tender, about 30 minutes. Drain any leftover broth. Toss the lentils with the olive oil and garlic powder and spread into one layer on one lined baking sheet. Set aside.

prep the candied parsnips

Lay the parsnips on the second baking sheet. In a small bowl, whisk together the maple syrup, olive oil, and brown sugar. Pour all over the parsnips and give them a good toss to coat them well.

Bake the lentils and parsnips for 20 to 30 minutes, giving the lentils a good shake after 10 minutes to ensure even browning. The lentils are done when crispy and the parsnips are done when tender, golden brown, and the edges look crispy.

make the pureed cannellini

Heat the lemon oil in a medium saucepan over medium heat. Add the shallot and garlic and sauté until softened. Transfer to a food processor or high-powered blender and add the cannellini beans, lemon zest and juice, and salt. Puree all ingredients together. Return the pureed mixture to the saucepan to warm before serving.

When everything is ready, serve by making a bed of the puree on a platter. Top with candied parsnips and crispy lentils. Finish with a drizzle of lemon olive oil.

soooo gouda quinoa + truffle bake

plant forward

ready in 45 minutes

serves 6

3 tablespoons extra-virgin olive oil + more for greasing dish

3½ cups chicken broth (or broth of choice)

2 cups uncooked quinoa

1 large sweet yellow onion, sliced

1 heaping cup cremini (or your favorite) mushrooms, roughly chopped

4 cloves fresh garlic, smashed, peeled, and chopped

3 to 4 teaspoons finely chopped fresh chives

1 teaspoon chopped fresh oregano

½ cup white wine of choice

1 cup low-fat Greek yogurt

1 cup shredded truffle Gouda cheese, divided

 **notes**

Quinoa seems to be one of those foods that has both loyal followers and haters. But this dish is a star, not just because quinoa is a complete plant-based protein, but because it's savory, cheesy, and delicious—and somehow brings everyone together. And it's a side that will make you want to skip the main dish!

Preheat the oven to 350°F. Grease a 9 x 13-inch baking dish with a little olive oil and set aside.

Bring the broth to a boil in a medium saucepan and add the quinoa. Stir well, reduce to a simmer, and cook until the quinoa is done and all the liquid is absorbed, about 15 minutes.

Heat the 3 tablespoons olive oil in a large skillet over medium heat. Add the onion and sauté until tender, about 5 minutes. Add the mushrooms, garlic, chives, and oregano, and stir until most of the moisture has evaporated. Add the wine carefully to avoid splashing an open flame, and stir to deglaze the pan. Remove from heat.

In a large mixing bowl, combine the quinoa, mushroom mixture, yogurt, and two-thirds of the cheese. Spread evenly into the baking dish and top with remaining cheese. (We never judge anyone who adds more cheese.) Bake until heated all the way through and the cheese is melted and slightly golden, about 15 minutes.

tip

This also makes great weekday lunches!

roasted beets

plant forward

ready in 1 hour, 10 minutes
serves 4

4 beets, any color
Extra-virgin olive oil
Garlic powder
Onion powder
Kosher salt
Pepper

 **notes**

The more color you add to your diet, the more health you add! Beets are rich in antioxidants, fiber, and folate—that's why it would be so sweet if you can learn to love the beet. These roasted beets might just be the road to getting you there. This is a simple approach that brings out the best in the beet and keeps the vegetable's natural crunchy texture. Beets are earthy, floral, buttery and sweet, great as a side or in salads.

Preheat the oven to 350°F.

Use a sharp paring knife to remove stems and peel the beets. Place each beet on a 12-inch piece of foil and drizzle with olive oil to coat. Sprinkle garlic powder, onion powder, salt, and pepper over each beet, ensuring they are thoroughly coated. Wrap each beet in foil.

Place the foil packs on a baking sheet and bake for 1 hour or until tender. Cool, then cut into ¼-inch slices or chunks.

tip

We like to peel the beets before baking because it saves the step of washing them, and they're easier to manage (with messy red hands) when they are raw than when they are hot.

lemony sautéed spinach

plant forward

ready in 10 minutes
serves 4

3 tablespoons extra-virgin
   olive oil
2 large shallots, sliced thin
5 cloves fresh garlic,
   smashed, peeled,
   and chopped
1 pound (about 10 cups
   or 10 giant handfuls)
   fresh baby spinach
Kosher salt and freshly
   ground black pepper
Fresh lemon wedge
   to squeeze

notes

From breakfast smoothies to salads to easy sautés, baby spinach is such a versatile standby that we keep a big container in the fridge. Sautéed spinach is high in nutrition and yum factor, and delightfully easy: It whips up in less than five minutes! We have converted many "cooked-spinach haters" with this recipe.

In a large skillet or wok, heat the olive oil over medium-high heat. Add the shallots and garlic and sauté until the shallots have softened and the garlic has infused into the oil, 3 to 4 minutes. (Be careful not to burn the garlic; reduce the heat if necessary.) Add the spinach then salt and pepper to taste, and cook and toss until the spinach softens or wilts—this happens very quickly, 1 to 2 minutes. Finish with a good squeeze of lemon.

tip

We like the spinach to still have a little bit of texture—not too soggy and retain a bright green color. One or two minutes should be perfect for wilting without the mush or slime. We want even the kids to love this dish ... and they will!

creamy, dreamy, cheesy polenta

ready in 30 minutes

serves 4

3 cups chicken broth

4 fresh cloves garlic,
    smashed and peeled

1 cup polenta (corn grits)

3 tablespoons
    unsalted butter

1 cup heavy cream

½ cup grated Parmesan
    cheese (or your favorite)

 **notes**

Polenta is a dreamy dish! Many refer to it as Italian grits, but we have fun calling it cheesy porridge. It's definitely one of those magical dishes that allows you to create a texture and flavor to enhance any dish. It can be a side to (or a bed for) just about anything. We love to drag succulent shrimp, braised short ribs, a good steak, or a juicy pork chop right through a pile of polenta for the most dreamy bites.

In a large saucepan, bring the broth and garlic cloves to a boil. Whisk in the polenta and reduce the heat. Cook slowly, stirring occasionally or until the liquid is gone, about 20 minutes. Add the butter and stir until melted and combined. Add the cream and Parm, stirring until the polenta is warm again, less than a minute.

tips

- We use all kinds of cheeses in our polenta. Base your choice on the main dish: Shrimp and grits? How about 1 cup sharp cheddar (see Shrimp + Grits recipe, page 230). Steak? We like ⅓ cup goat cheese.
- A fried egg on top of polenta leftovers makes a dreamy breakfast!

cheesy lemon asparagus

ready in 25 to 30 minutes
serves 4

1 bunch asparagus, trimmed
Extra-virgin olive oil
Garlic powder
1 small lemon, cut in half
Shredded Gruyère cheese
Kosher salt and freshly
    ground black
    pepper to taste

 **notes**

Such simplicity, such a star! Simply roasted asparagus is so tasty, it can completely stand on its own, but sometimes it's fun to take it to another level. "That's not better with cheese," said no one, ever! This recipe makes a superstar side dish or an exciting starter.

Preheat the oven to 400°F.

Lay the asparagus all in the same direction on a baking sheet. Drizzle with olive oil, sprinkle with garlic powder, and roll the spears around to coat. Spread to a single layer and squeeze lemon juice generously over all.

Roast asparagus for 10 to 15 minutes (depending on thickness)—they should be softened but still have some firm texture. Sprinkle on the Gruyère and return to the oven for another 2 to 3 minutes or until the cheese is melted and bubbly. Add salt and freshly ground black pepper to taste.

brown-buttered candied heirloom carrots

plant forward

ready in 35 minutes
serves 4 to 5

2 pounds colored
    heirloom carrots
2 tablespoons
    unsalted butter
3 cloves fresh garlic,
    smashed, peeled,
    and chopped
6 tablespoons packed
    dark brown sugar
¼ cup honey
1 tablespoon thick
    balsamic vinegar
1 sprig fresh rosemary
Kosher salt and freshly
    ground black
    pepper to taste
+ added yum:
    ¼ cup crushed nuts

 **notes**

This colorful, special carrot side comes together with little effort. It's gorgeous and tastes more like candy than vegetables.

Carrots are so good for us! Rich in beta carotene, vitamin K, fiber, and antioxidants, they are believed to slow down the aging process, keep us healthier by fighting infection, and prevent certain types of cancer. Add color to your world; add more carrots to your life!

Preheat the oven to 350°F.

Scrub the carrots, then cut thick carrots in half (leave smaller carrots whole). Melt the butter in a cast iron skillet over medium heat, then let it brown for 1 minute. Add the garlic and sauté for 1 minute. Remove from heat and add the brown sugar, honey, and balsamic vinegar and mix well. Add the carrots and rosemary and rotate the carrots to coat with the mixture. Transfer the skillet to the oven and roast until the carrots are tender, 22 to 25 minutes. Season with salt and pepper.

+ added yum: Sprinkle with toasted nuts of choice. We love hazelnuts, walnuts, and pecans.

tip

If you don't have an oven-safe skillet, use a shallow baking dish. Just mix all ingredients with the browned butter in a bowl, then toss with carrots.

roasted fingerling potatoes + fennel + parm

ready in 40 minutes

serves 3 to 4

1 pound fingerling potatoes

2 small fennel bulbs

⅓ cup extra-virgin olive oil

Kosher salt and
    pepper to taste

½ cup freshly grated
    Parmesan cheese

 **notes**

Fennel is fun! Something very magical happens to fennel when you roast it. It loses its licorice flavor and melts into a caramelized, sweet, and buttery companion to roasted potatoes. It's hard to explain, but it adds an elegance and a touch of sophistication that will make you proud to serve the dish to company on special occasions. We love a simple recipe with fresh ingredients that feels so elevated!

Preheat the oven 425°F.

Cut the fingerling potatoes in half lengthwise and place face down on a baking sheet. Cut the green tops off the fennel bulbs, then into six slim wedges. (Be sure to cut through the core to help keep wedges in one piece.)

Place the fennel wedges on the baking sheet with potatoes and drizzle both with the olive oil. Sprinkle with salt and pepper. Toss well with your hands to coat evenly. Roast the vegetables for 25 minutes (toss them about halfway through) or until the potatoes are soft, golden, and crisp. Sprinkle the Parmesan over everything and roast for 2 minutes longer or until the cheese melts.

home fries

ready in 15 to 20 minutes
serves 6

Vegetable oil for frying
1 (32-ounce) bag frozen
   steak fries
Kosher salt

 **notes**

Is there anyone in the world who doesn't sometimes crave really fresh, hot, delicious french fries? How often do you order them in a restaurant with great excitement and anticipation, only for them to arrive soggy or cold? Getting comfortable working with a vat of hot oil and making fries at home will empower and delight you.

In a large Dutch oven, heat at least 3 inches of oil over medium-high heat until it registers 350°F on a deep-fry or candy thermometer. Use a spider spoon to safely lower the fries into the hot oil. Fry for 10 to 15 minutes, gently stirring occasionally to help the fries cook evenly, until golden brown. The fries will start to float a bit when they are done. Carefully lift fries with a spider spoon and transfer to a baking sheet or platter lined with paper towels. Sprinkle with kosher or truffle salt.

tips

- The temperature of the oil will drop when you add the fries. The fries will take about 10 minutes to cook once the temperature returns to 350°F.
- We love truffle everything. Try adding truffle salt to fries instead of regular kosher salt.

cumin + cotija street fries

ready in 15 minutes

serves 6

Vegetable oil for frying

1 (28-ounce) bag frozen
    shoestring fries

½ cup cotija cheese

Ground cumin (enough for
    a nice sprinkle)

Kosher salt and
    pepper to taste

¼ cup chopped fresh cilantro

 **notes**

These street fries, more inspiration than recipe (but still exciting!), make a great side or festive snack. Any friend grabbing a stool at your kitchen counter is sure to be excited when you tell them you're whipping up some fresh fries for their meal or as a little snack to go with drinks. It's fun to mix up potato types, shapes, sizes, and spices. The fries make a great side to our Bistec de Pollo (page 188), Barbacoa Beef (page 225), and Mojo Pulled Pork (page 273)—or as a fun snack with some margaritas!

Heat at least 3 inches of oil in a large Dutch oven over medium-high heat until it registers 350°F on a deep-fry or candy thermometer. Use a spider spoon to safely lower the fries into the hot oil. Fry for about 10 minutes, gently stirring occasionally to help the fries cook evenly, until golden brown. The fries will start to float a bit when they are done.

Carefully lift out the fries with a spider spoon and transfer to a baking sheet or platter lined with paper towels. Sprinkle immediately with the cotija and cumin. Season with salt and pepper to taste, garnish with cilantro, and serve.

grilled zucchini + dusted parm

plant forward

ready in 10 minutes
serves 4 to 6

4 medium zucchini, trimmed
1 tablespoon extra-virgin
   olive oil
½ teaspoon paprika
½ teaspoon garlic powder
½ teaspoon onion powder
¼ cup grated Parmesan
   cheese, plus more
   for + added yum
Kosher salt and freshly
   ground black
   pepper to taste

+ added yum:
   grated Parmesan cheese

We have found that sometimes, the simplest recipes can be the tastiest and most satisfying. Learning to perfect vegetables is like finding a favorite way to move your body: eventually, you're doing it all of the time and it's just because you enjoy the goodness it brings to your life. Grilled zucchini allows you to find the texture you enjoy, and the charred and cheesy flavors combined will have you making this easy side all of the time!

Preheat a grill to medium-high.

Slice the zucchini in half lengthwise and in half lengthwise again to create long strips. Brush with olive oil on both flesh sides. Sprinkle flesh sides with the paprika, garlic powder, onion powder, and then the Parmesan. Grill for 2 to 3 minutes with the cover on, flip them and cook for another 2 to 3 minutes or until charred and tender but not limp and mushy. Sprinkle with salt and pepper to taste.

+ added yum: Sprinkle with an additional good dose of grated Parmesan cheese while the zucchini is hot.

 **notes**

russet + sweet potato mashup

ready in 30 to 35 minutes

serves 5 to 6

3 russet potatoes

3 sweet potatoes

Cold water, enough to
    cover potatoes

Kosher salt

4 tablespoons
    unsalted butter

4 cloves fresh garlic,
    smashed, peeled,
    and chopped

1½ cups heavy
    whipping cream

♡ notes

Make a weeknight meal feel holiday special with this potato lovers' mashup. You will wonder how you've lived without it in your life. It is so perfect for the drag many of us love to do with a piece of salmon or meat. Yummm! A Thanksgiving turkey would also be proud to have this by its side.

Peel the russet potatoes and sweet potatoes and cut into pieces, making sure all piece sizes are similar so they cook evenly. Place the potatoes in a large stockpot, add cold water to cover, and add a good pinch of salt. Bring to boil, reduce the heat, and simmer for 15 to 20 minutes or until tender. Drain and set potatoes aside in a large bowl.

Heat the butter and garlic in the stockpot over medium heat. When butter is browned (about 1 minute), add the cream and cook until warmed through. Pour the cream mixture over the potatoes and use a hand masher to mash to your desired consistency. We like it a little chunky.

cheat sheet pan-roasted veggies inspo

ready in 45 minutes

serves 4 to 5

12 medium Brussels
    sprouts, halved

1 zucchini, chopped

8 asparagus spears, trimmed

3 to 4 large leaves collard
    greens or kale

1 fennel bulb, trimmed,
    cored, and sliced

3 tablespoons extra-virgin
    olive oil

Garlic powder to taste

Onion powder to taste

Kosher salt and ground
    black pepper to taste

1½ tablespoons thick
    balsamic vinegar or glaze

½ lemon

notes

These cheat sheet recipes are really just inspiration for you, rather than some brand-new recipe. Every Peddie daughter first started cooking by learning a simple roasted vegetable recipe. We call them cheat sheets because roasting a big sheet pan of veggies creates such a bountiful, easy meal, you feel like you're cheating the system somehow.

Preheat the oven to 425°F.

Cut the veggies in shapes/sizes that will allow all of them to roast evenly. Place on a large baking sheet, drizzle with olive oil, and toss but keep veggies separate. Sprinkle on garlic powder and onion powder, to taste, then season with salt and pepper. Toss again, keeping them separate. Drizzle the Brussel sprouts and zucchini with balsamic glaze. Roast until desired tenderness and color, 20 to 25 minutes. Squeeze lemon all over right before serving.

tips

- Add any other green veggies you love or fresh herbs you have on hand.
- The beauty of these sheet pan veggies is you can prep the sheet ahead and pop it in the oven just before dinner.

variation
cheat sheet roasted red + orange veggies inspo

Go to town with red and orange veggies, following the cheat sheet above, but substituting any or all of the following:

- Tricolored carrots (halved lengthwise)
- Red beets (cubed)
- Yellow beets (cubed)
- Parsnips (trimmed and halved)
- Small red potatoes (whole, or halved if large)
- Red onions (sliced)

applesauce

ready in 40 minutes
makes about 3 Mason jars

12 apples, any variety or
    combination, peeled and
    cored (or chopped)
1½ cups apple juice
Juice of 1 small lemon
1 teaspoon unsalted butter
½ cup packed dark
    brown sugar
1 teaspoon ground cinnamon

 **notes**

Any Brady Bunch fans out there? Remember Bobby Brady's catchphrase when he was practicing his Humphrey Bogart impression? If you're familiar with it, then you know it's almost impossible to not say "pork chopsh and appleshauuce" just like Bobby. (Search it if you need a smile.) Serve the applesauce with Pork Chops for the Applesauce (page 222).

In addition to being a partner to pork chopsh, the appleshauuce makes a great snack and is delicious on oatmeal.

Combine all the ingredients in a large saucepan. Bring to a boil, reduce the heat, cover, and simmer for 25 minutes. Stir occasionally and check for enough liquid, adding more apple juice if needed. The apples are done when you can easily mash one with a large spoon. Use an immersion blender or food processor to puree and blend well. Pour into Mason jars or serving bowl and refrigerate to chill. Refrigerate up to one week.

tips

- Have extra apple juice on hand in case you need more liquid to make the apples softer.
- Different apples may require longer cooking times.

butter bean, grilled corn + zucchini omg bowl

plant forward

ready in 1 hour, 15 minutes
serves 4 to 6

2 tablespoons lemon
     extra-virgin olive oil

1 tablespoon honey

1 teaspoon grated lemon
     zest + 2 tablespoons juice
     (from 1 large lemon)

1 large clove fresh
     garlic, grated fine

Leaves from 1 sprig
     fresh thyme

Freshly ground black pepper

1 (15.5-can) cannellini beans,
     drained and rinsed

1 (15.5-can) butter beans,
     drained and rinsed

1 large zucchini

2 cups (3 to 4 ears)
     grilled corn kernels
     (see Tips), cooled

2 tablespoons pecans

½ cup fresh chopped basil

♡ **notes**

We love a good, omg! side that can also serve as nutritious and delicious lunches for the week. This bean, zucchini, and corn dish is light and bright, yet so satisfying and hearty. The textures and flavors all work so well together; it feels like sunshine going into your body! We hope this dish inspires you to add nuts to more dishes. They provide plant-based protein, fiber, and heart-healthy fats—not to mention more crunch to munch. This will surely be a favorite!

In a large mixing bowl, whisk together the olive oil, honey, lemon zest and juice, garlic, thyme, and a twist of black pepper. Mix in the cannellini and butter beans and let marinate for an hour.

Cut the zucchini in half. Then slice each half lengthwise and cut those in half again to make eight spears. Cut each spear into thin triangles.

Add the zucchini, corn, pecans, basil, and 2 big twists of black pepper to the bean mixture. Mix well and serve!

tips

- If you don't have time to marinate the beans, it's still delicious; don't skip this recipe because of it. But honestly, this is even better as it sits so you can make ahead of time!
- See the Grilled Corn, Corn, Corn Chicken Chowder recipe (pages 68–69) for grilling corn on the cob instructions. You'll need 3 or 4 ears of corn here to yield the 2 cups corn kernels. When cooled, cut the corn off very close to the cob, allowing blocks of corn to stay together. It makes for a yummy bite and pretty presentation.

sexy slow cooker good-luck black-eyed peas

Prep is 20 minutes
ready in 4 hours
serves 4 to 6

4 slices bacon

¼ cup extra-virgin olive oil

1 medium red onion,
chopped fine

1 red bell pepper, cored,
seeded, and chopped fine

1 yellow bell pepper, cored,
seeded, and chopped fine

4 cloves fresh garlic,
smashed, peeled,
and chopped

3 (15-ounce) cans black-eyed
peas, drained halfway

2 bay leaves

1 tablespoon fresh
thyme leaves

 **notes**

My dad passed down the tradition of making black-eyed peas on New Year's Day to ring in the new year with good luck and prosperity. His Southern roots insisted we serve it with cornbread (page 173) and collard greens (page 177). As the tradition goes, the black-eyed peas represent coins, the greens represent paper money, and the cornbread represents gold.

When I was a kid, cornbread was about the only part of this meal I enjoyed, but now it's one of my favorite meals—and I eat it year-round. It's very comforting and nutritious.

Black-eyed peas are a good source of magnesium, which supports muscle and nerve function.

I like making them in the slow cooker because I'm often taking down Christmas decor on New Year's Day. I know I have my good luck for the year cooking while I'm busy working!

—Sharon

Turn the slow cooker on high and arrange the bacon to cover the bottom. Add the oil, cover the cooker, and cook for 1 hour.

Add the onion, peppers, and garlic. Cover and cook for 1 hour.

Drain half of the liquid from the cans and add the black-eyed peas, bay leaves, and thyme. Reduce the heat to low and cook for 2 hours.

tips

- It's perfectly OK to add all ingredients at the same time if you will not be around for the gradual stages.
- You don't have to cook the bacon in its own step; although it does give the bacon a more desirable texture and color, it's the flavor it adds that we are after.

sweet southern cornbread

tradition

ready in 40 minutes

serves 8

1¼ cups yellow cornmeal

1½ cups all-purpose
flour of choice

1 cup sugar

2 teaspoons baking powder

¼ teaspoon baking soda

1 teaspoon kosher salt

4 eggs

1½ cups milk

⅓ cup vegetable oil

+ added yum:

1½ cups frozen yellow
corn and 1 cup shredded
sharp cheddar cheese

 **notes**

Growing up on Southern cornbread made us love sweeter cornbread, but let's be real: There's no such thing as bad cornbread. This Southern variety has a buttery, cakelike texture and we just love its cozy, home-sweet-home vibes. It's comforting and delicious, especially when you add the extra love and yum.

Of course, cornbread is the perfect addition to the new year's good luck tradition of black-eyed peas (Sexy Slow Cooker Good-Luck Black-Eyed Peas page 170) and sautéed Not-Your-Grandma's Collard Greens (page 177), but it also makes a wonderful, warm companion to soups, stews, and chili.

Preheat the oven to 375°F. Grease an 8-inch square baking pan.

In a medium bowl, combine the cornmeal, flour, sugar, baking powder, baking soda, and salt. In a standing mixer or other large bowl with an electric mixer, whisk the eggs, milk, and oil. While mixing, slowly add the dry mixture to the liquid and mix until well combined. If you like, add the corn and cheddar (**+ added yum**) now to give the cornbread a little extra love. Scrape the batter into the prepared pan. Bake for 30 minutes or until a toothpick inserted in the center comes out clean.

tip

Try serving it with soft butter and a drizzle of honey.

southern cornbread dressing

tradition ♥

ready in 1 hour, 10 minutes
serves 8 to 10

½ cup (1 stick) unsalted butter
2 cups chopped yellow onion
2 cups chopped celery
2 tablespoons chopped
fresh sage
2 tablespoons fresh
rosemary needles
2 tablespoons chopped
fresh parsley
Leaves of 10 sprigs
fresh thyme
½ teaspoon dried oregano
½ teaspoon kosher salt
Fresh ground pepper
4 cloves fresh garlic,
smashed, peeled,
and chopped fine
Cornbread (see Tip)
3 cups chicken broth
2 eggs

♥ notes

So this is one of those family recipes that has changed a bit over the years depending on who is making it. That's one of the best things about recipes—the people who make them can add their own special touches based on tastes, allergies, etc. The one thing that will never change in the Southern side of our family and our homes is that turkey's tastiest best friend is "dressing," not "stuffing." And dressing means cornbread must be the base. Breadcrumb stuffing with breadcrumbs is good, but cornbread dressing is the most buttery, tasty, and savory—at least in our Southern brainwashed opinions. This cornbread dressing will create nostalgia and always feel like family and beautiful memories, no matter who makes it.

Preheat the oven to 375°F. Grease a 9 x 13-inch baking dish.

Melt the butter in a large stockpot over medium heat. Add the onions, celery, and herbs and season with salt and pepper. Cook until translucent, 6 to 8 minutes. Add the garlic and sauté for another minute. Remove from heat.

Crumble the cornbread into the pot and combine well. In a mixing bowl, whisk the broth and eggs. Add to cornbread mixture and work with your hands to incorporate all the ingredients. Drop and spread into the prepared baking dish. Bake for 40 minutes or until heated through and lightly toasted on top.

tip

Make your favorite cornbread in a 9 x 13-inch pan according to package instructions and let cool. Or use our Sweet Southern Cornbread (page 173), but leave out the corn and cheddar, and bake it in a 9 x 13-inch pan at 350°F for 30 minutes.

not-your-grandma's collard greens

ready in 15 minutes
serves 2 to 3

1 bunch collard greens
3 tablespoons extra-virgin
   olive oil
1 shallot (2 bulbs) or 1 small
   red onion, sliced thin
3 fresh cloves garlic,
   smashed, peeled,
   and chopped
½ to 1 tablespoon sriracha
Kosher salt and fresh
   ground pepper

 **notes**

Too often, you hear adults say they don't like vegetables. And the truth is, even though we know vegetables are good for us, few of us probably eat as many as we should. Most likely, it's because of the way a particular vegetable was prepared. We bet if you asked most people if they'd like some collard greens, they'd say no thanks, thinking of their grandmother pushing the mushy vegetables. Our collard green recipe is modern, bright, and just the right texture. We hope you'll give these collard greens a try; you'll feel like you are adulting at your highest level!

Wash the collard greens well in warm water and let drain. Rip the leaves off the fat part of the stems and discard the stems. You can leave the soft part of the higher stem on top. Fold the leaf in half, slice down the middle of the leaf lengthwise. Stack the halves on top of each other and cut crosswise in approximately 1-inch pieces.

In a large skillet or wok, heat the oil over medium-high heat. Add the shallot and cook until translucent. Add the garlic and cook less than a minute to flavor the oil. Then quickly add the collard greens and sauté for 3 to 4 minutes. You want them to be bright green and soft, but still with some texture. No dark, mushy, icky greens coming from your kitchen; we want fresh and bright! Shut off the heat, add the sriracha, salt, and pepper, give another quick stir, and you're ready to serve!

tips

- They cook quickly, so be careful not to overcook.
- They are perfect as a weeknight, green side dish. They are also representative of good fortune for a new year! We serve them on New Year's Day with our Sexy Slow Cooker Good-Luck Black-Eyed Peas (page 170) and Sweet Southern Cornbread (page 173) to ring in the new year.

oven-baked sweet potato fries

plant forward

ready in 30 to 35 minutes
serves 4 to 6, depending
on potato size

4 sweet potatoes
3 tablespoons cornstarch
1 teaspoon ground cumin
1 teaspoon kosher salt,
    plus more to taste
1 teaspoon black pepper,
    plus more to taste
½ cup extra-virgin olive oil

 **notes**

Learning to make your own crispy, addictive, baked sweet potato fries will be one of the sweetest gifts you'll give yourself and your family. The sweet potatoes are a healthier alternative to regular fries and delicious as a side or snack. It's also fun to experiment with different spices each time you make them.

Preheat the oven to 425°F. Line two large baking sheets with parchment paper.

Scrub the potatoes well but leave the skins on. Cut off the ends and a little bit from each side so the potato can rest evenly on each side. Cut into ¼-inch fry shapes.

In a large, resealable plastic bag, combine the cornstarch, cumin, salt, and pepper. Shake it well to mix. Add the potato fries and shake well to coat them. Lift the fries out of the bag by hand, shaking off the excess cornstarch mixture and transfer to a large bowl.

Drizzle the potatoes with the olive oil and toss to coat. Spread them out on the baking sheets with pieces not touching to prevent steaming and ensure crispiness. (We use two sheets to spread them out and ensure every fry is crispy.) Bake for 15 minutes. Use a spatula to flip each fry over. Rotate the pans and bake for another 10 to 15 minutes or until browned and crispy. Watch closely for the last 5 minutes. Season with additional salt and pepper and serve immediately to preserve crispiness.

aioli our way

1 cup sour cream

1 tablespoon extra-virgin
   olive oil

1 teaspoon paprika

1 teaspoon garlic powder

½ teaspoon truffle salt

Juice of ½ lemon

¼ cup grated Parmesan
   cheese

Kosher salt and freshly
   ground black
   pepper to taste

 **notes**

A classic aioli is made of garlic, olive oil, and eggs, plus or minus a few other ingredients depending on who's making it. Problem is, half of our family hates mayo, and the classic combination is pretty much mayonnaise. We're all big dippers, so over the years, we've made everyone happy by coming up with "aioli our way." Really, we're not sure it should even be called "aioli," but it's a great impostor and gives you that same rich dipping sauce vibe. It is creamy, garlicky, and luxurious for french fries and tater tots!

Mix all ingredients well and, *poof!* there it is.

tip

Kelsey likes to throw a little truffle oil into her aioli. Try adding about ½ tablespoon for an added kick of truffle.

quick + easy cuban-style black beans

ready in 25 minutes

serves 5 to 6

3 tablespoons extra-virgin olive oil

1 green bell pepper, cored, seeded, and chopped

1 small yellow onion, chopped fine

3 cloves fresh garlic, smashed, peeled, and chopped

2 (15-ounce) cans black beans (we love Goya brand), not drained

½ teaspoon garlic powder

¼ teaspoon onion powder

½ teaspoon dried oregano

Kosher salt + freshly ground black pepper to taste

Growing up in South Florida, it was easy to find Cuban black beans in a can. Depending on where you live, it may not be so easy, but it's pretty easy to duplicate the flavors with this quick recipe. It's simple and you won't believe how this takes black beans to a whole new level of delishness!

Heat the olive oil in a medium saucepan over medium heat. Add the pepper, onion, and garlic and cook for 2 to 3 minutes or until the onions are translucent. Add the beans, garlic powder, onion powder, and oregano and simmer for 15 minutes or until the flavors have a chance to come together.

Scoop out 1 cup of the beans, transfer to a bowl, and mash with a potato masher or the back of a fork. Return them to the pot and let simmer for a few more minutes or until the mixture looks cloudy and thick. Season with salt and pepper to taste and serve.

 **notes**

these will get you to love brussels sprouts

ready in 20 minutes

serves 4 to 5

20 small Brussels sprouts

¼ cup extra-virgin olive oil

2 cloves fresh garlic,
    smashed, peeled,
    and chopped

1 (5-ounce) package
    uncured, diced pancetta

Kosher salt and freshly
    ground black
    pepper to taste

1 tablespoon balsamic glaze

 **notes**

Brussels sprouts are a staple in our family. Sure, they have a bit of a bad reputation, but that's because old recipes produced mushy and unexciting sprouts. Cooked up quick and crispy, they have a naturally nutty, earthy flavor and fun texture. We have experimented with roasted and air-fried Brussels, but throwing them in a cast iron pan on the stove makes for a quick side on a weeknight or a bright pairing for a weekend dinner party.

Brussels sprouts are Kelsey's favorite vegetable, so she decided to grow some in her garden this year. We'll be sneaking over to her house to steal some.

Trim the hard stem off the top of each sprout, remove the outside leaves, and cut in half. Heat the oil in a cast iron pan over medium-high heat. Place the sprouts in the pan cut side down. Add the garlic and pancetta. Cook for 5 minutes, then flip the sprouts and move around the pancetta. Cook for 5 more minutes or until charred and tender. Drizzle with a thick, balsamic glaze, stir, and serve.

family dinners *sunday*

The positive and lasting effects of the family dinner table should not be underestimated. It's where strong individuals and crucial bonds are built, where empathy for family members and valuable listening skills are taught, and where teamwork and table manners are learned and polished. It has been our family philosophy that no matter how busy the rest of the week is, Sunday dinner as a family is a priority. It's a commitment to come together, a cherished time to create a civilized meal, sit down, regroup, and get each other centered for the upcoming week. On Sunday nights, we either make favorite family recipes like these, or try out new ones on each other.

bistec de pollo

4 boneless, skinless
   chicken breasts

2 teaspoons ground cumin

1½ teaspoons dried oregano

1 teaspoon garlic powder

½ teaspoon ground allspice

1 teaspoon kosher salt

1 teaspoon freshly ground
   black pepper

4 tablespoons extra-virgin
   olive oil, divided

4 tablespoons unsalted
   butter, divided

2 onions, sliced

8 cloves fresh garlic,
   smashed, peeled,
   and chopped

2 small limes, cut into wedges

 **notes**

Growing up in South Florida, Sharon's favorite kind of food to eat out was Cuban food. She lost access to it when she moved to Oregon, so she learned to make some of her favorites. Bistec de pollo is a beloved Cuban classic. As you smell the nutty, earthy, and buttery spices join together with the onions and garlic, you won't be able to get the tender, beautifully golden chicken on your table fast enough. Cubans know how to cook with love and flavor, and this recipe will make you homesick for places you've never even been. Serve with Quick + Easy Cuban-Style Black Beans (page 182), Cumin + Cotija Street Fries (page 158), or your favorite white rice.

Place a chicken breast on a steady cutting surface. Cut in half horizontally by holding a long sharp knife along the long side of the chicken breast and begin carefully moving the knife back and forth through it like a saw. Repeat with the remaining breasts. Cover with parchment paper and pound each piece with a meat mallet until it is about ¼ inch thick.

Combine the cumin, oregano, garlic powder, allspice, salt, and pepper in a small bowl. Coat chicken on both sides with the spice mix. Heat 2 tablespoons of the oil and 2 tablespoons of the butter in a large skillet over medium heat. Add the chicken and cook for 3 to 4 minutes on each side or until golden brown and cooked through. Remove the chicken and cover with foil to keep warm.

Add the remaining oil and butter, the onions, and garlic to the skillet and cook for 5 to 7 minutes or until the onions are until browned and softened. Return the chicken to the skillet and squeeze lime over all. Move everything around, burying the chicken in the onions. Ready to serve!

oodles of zoodles (+ savory lentil "meatballs")

Zoodles are a fun and delicious alternative to pasta. We love them with savory lentil "meatballs" (next page) for a bright, bold meatless meal packed full of health and color!

ready in 20 minutes

serves 4

2 tablespoons extra-virgin
olive oil

1 bell pepper of choice, cored,
seeded, and sliced in strips

2 cloves fresh garlic,
smashed, peeled,
and minced

4 zucchini or 1 butternut
squash, spiralized

½ teaspoon kosher salt

Freshly ground black pepper

Savory Lentil "Meatballs"
(recipe next page)

+ added yum:
½ cup fresh grated
Parmesan cheese

Heat the olive oil in a large skillet. Add the pepper and garlic and sauté until almost soft, 2 to 3 minutes. Add zucchini or butternut squash noodles and cook until slightly tender but still crunchy, 3 to 4 minutes. Season with salt and pepper and serve with "meatballs" on top, if desired.

+ added yum: Sprinkle fresh Parmesan cheese on top!

tip

The recipe is delicious with either zucchini or butternut squash noodles, but zucchini is much easier to spiralize. If you can buy the squash already in noodles, it's a lot more convenient.

 **notes**

savory lentil "meatballs"

ready in 1 hour
makes 8 to 12 balls

2 tablespoons +
    1 teaspoon extra-virgin
    olive oil, divided
1 shallot, chopped fine
4 cloves fresh garlic,
    smashed, peeled,
    and chopped fine
1½ cups dry lentils,
    cooked according to
    package instructions
1 egg
⅔ cup grated Parmesan
    cheese
¼ cup chopped fresh parsley
2 tablespoons tomato paste
1 tablespoon panko crumbs
    (gluten-free OK)
⅛ teaspoon dried oregano
Salt and freshly ground
    black pepper

 **notes**

These "meatballs" are savory, rich, and packed full of fiber and protein—perfect for a meatless Monday. Yeah, they're not trying to be your Italian grandmother's meatballs, but they are so satisfying and a great way to keep expanding your nutrition portfolio. We love them on top of oodles of zoodles (see recipe previous page) and they're great with marinara sauce and additional Parm. They also make super snacks.

Preheat the oven to 375°F. Line a baking sheet with parchment paper.

In a large skillet over medium heat, heat 2 tablespoons of olive oil. Add the shallot and garlic and sauté for 2 to 3 minutes or until slightly golden brown.

Transfer the shallot and garlic to a food processor and add the cooked lentils, 1 teaspoon olive oil, egg, Parmesan, parsley, tomato paste, panko, oregano, and salt and pepper to taste. Pulse well until well combined. Scrape the mixture into a bowl.

Using a cookie dough scoop, make balls from the mixture and place on the lined baking sheet. (The size of the balls determines whether this recipe yields 8, 10, or 12 meatballs.) Bake for 10 to 15 minutes or until the meatballs are golden.

cod + veggies fish foils

complete meal

ready in 30 minutes

serves 4

compound butter

4 tablespoons unsalted
    butter, softened

4 large cloves garlic, grated

2 teaspoons grated
    lemon zest

2 teaspoons fresh
    thyme leaves

Kosher salt and freshly
    ground black
    pepper to taste

fish packets

20 small tricolored potatoes,
    sliced very thin

4 medium carrots, peeled and
    cut in very thin matchsticks

2 small fennel bulbs,
    sliced very thin

¼ cup white wine

Kosher salt and freshly
    ground black pepper

4 (6-ounce) pieces cod
    or white fish
    (1- to 1½-inches thick)

1 lemon, cut into 4 wedges

¼ cup chopped fresh parsley

We love fish foils for many reasons. They're so cute and fun and there are no pots and pans to clean up after. In addition, the foil protects the delicate fish, keeping it moist and savory and providing the veggies with wonderful texture and loads of flavor. Fish and veggie combinations are endless. Following are two of our favorites, but we could seriously keep going. The recipes serve four but are easy to scale up or down when you're serving family, a crowd, or just yourself.

Adjust your oven rack to the middle position and preheat the oven to 450°F. Cut out eight 12-inch foil squares.

make the compound butter

Combine all the ingredients in a bowl. Stir well and set aside.

make the fish packets

Microwave the potato slices in a medium bowl covered in plastic wrap for 2 minutes or until slightly softened.

In a medium bowl, combine the potatoes, carrots, fennel, wine, and salt and pepper to taste. Divide the veggies evenly among four foil squares. If there's liquid left at the bottom of the bowl, drizzle it over the veggies. Pat the fish dry and season with salt and pepper. Lay the fish on top of the veggies. Spread one-fourth of the compound butter mixture onto each piece of fish. Cover each pile of veggies and fish with a second piece of foil and fold the edges together a few times to make packets approximately 7-inches square.

Place the packets on a baking sheet and bake for 15 minutes. Be careful of the steam when you open foil. After plating, squeeze lemon over each one and top with chopped parsley.

tips

- You can assemble the packets an hour or two before baking if you're having company.
- Halibut or snapper are also delicious in this recipe.

mediterranean cod fish foils

complete meal

ready in 30 minutes
serves 4

flavored oil

¼ cup extra-virgin olive oil
4 large cloves fresh garlic,
    smashed, peeled,
    and chopped
2 teaspoons grated lemon zest
½ teaspoon fresh thyme leaves
½ teaspoon dried oregano
½ teaspoon kosher salt
½ teaspoon freshly ground
    black pepper

fish packets

2 pounds small tricolored
    potatoes, sliced very thin
1 pound green beans
1 (6-ounce) jar Greek olives,
    roughly chopped
1 (10-ounce) package
    cherry tomatoes
¼ cup capers
2 shallots, sliced thinly
¼ cup white wine
Kosher salt and freshly
    ground black pepper
4 (5- to 6-ounce) pieces cod
    or another firm white fish
    (1- to 1½-inches thick)
1 large lemon, cut
    into 4 wedges
¼ cup chopped fresh basil

Adjust your oven rack to the middle position and preheat to 450°F. Cut out eight 12-inch foil squares.

make the flavored oil

Combine all the ingredients together in a small bowl. Whisk together and set aside.

make the fish packets

Microwave the potato slices in a medium bowl covered in plastic wrap for 2 minutes or until slightly softened.

In a medium bowl, combine the potatoes, green beans, olives, tomatoes, capers, shallots, wine, and salt and pepper to taste. Divide the veggies evenly among four foil squares. If there's liquid left at the bottom of the bowl, drizzle it over the veggies. Pat the fish dry and season with salt and pepper. Lay one piece of fish on top of each pile of veggies and drizzle with one-fourth of the flavored oil. Cover each with a second piece of foil and fold the edges together a few times to make packets approximately 7-inches square.

Place the packets on a baking sheet and bake for 15 minutes. Be careful of the steam when you open foil. After plating, squeeze lemon over each one and top with basil.

tips

- You can assemble the packets an hour or two before baking if you're having company.
- Halibut or snapper are also delicious in this recipe.

 **notes**

bean + lentil pretty power bowls

ready in 35 minutes

serves 6 to 8

1 cup dry lentils

3 tablespoons extra-virgin
olive oil

1 large shallot, chopped

1 sweet red bell pepper, cored,
seeded, and chopped

1 sweet orange bell
pepper, cored, seeded,
and chopped

2 to 3 cloves fresh garlic,
smashed, peeled,
and chopped

Handful chopped fresh herbs
of choice (we love basil,
parsley, and cilantro in this)

1 teaspoon ground cardamom

1 teaspoon ground turmeric

Freshly ground black pepper

2 cups chopped stemmed
fresh kale

2 giant handfuls fresh spinach

1 (15.5-ounce) can garbanzo
beans, drained

1 (15.5-ounce) can black-
eyed peas, drained

Juice of ½ lemon

+ added yum:
Freshly grated
Parmesan cheese

This dish was born after the holidays one year when we were hustled, bustled, sugared out, and in need of some good-mood food. The colorful, nutrition-packed power bowls quickly became a regular staple, not just for dinners, but lunches too! As you're chopping the vegetables and seeing all of the beautiful colors coming together, you will immediately start thanking yourself for making such a nurturing, self-care dish. Loving yourself never tasted and felt so good.

Note that this is really more of an "ish" type recipe—throw in whatever veggies you have in whatever amounts you have.

Prepare the lentils according to package instructions. For added flavor, use vegetable or chicken broth instead of water.

Heat the olive oil in a wok or large skillet over medium-high heat. Add the shallot, bell peppers, and garlic and cook, stirring until the shallots are translucent and the peppers are at the desired texture, 5 to 7 minutes, depending on the size of your chop. We like to leave a little crunch on the peppers. Add the herbs, cardamom, turmeric, and black pepper, stirring well. Add the kale and spinach and toss well until they have softened,

Add the cooked lentils, garbanzos, and black-eyed peas and toss until heated through, 1 to 2 minutes. Remove from heat and squeeze fresh lemon juice all over.

+ added yum: Sprinkle freshly grated Parmesan cheese over the top.

 **notes**

beef + broccoli

complete meal

ready in 30 minutes

serves 4 to 5

2 pounds flat iron or
flank steak

⅔ cup + 2 teaspoons
cornstarch, divided

½ teaspoon garlic powder

½ teaspoon onion powder

¼ cup + 2 tablespoons
vegetable oil, divided

¾ cup packed brown sugar

⅔ cup soy sauce

½ cup water

4 or 5 scallions (white
and green parts),
sliced diagonally

4 cloves fresh garlic,
smashed, peeled,
and minced

1 teaspoon minced
fresh ginger

8 cups bite-size pieces
broccoli crowns

1½ cups cashews

Jasmine rice, cooked
according to package
instructions, for serving

Chinese beef and broccoli has been a family favorite at restaurants and takeout for years. You'll find that there are tons of beef/broc recipes online—ours is a combination of a lot of them, tweaked based on our preferences. We never feel like there are enough cashews, lol, so we are generous with our amount!

Cut the steak into very thin strips. In a resealable plastic bag, combine ⅔ cup cornstarch, the garlic powder, and onion powder. Shake well. Add the steak and shake well again to coat evenly.

Heat ¼ cup of the oil in a large skillet or sauté pan over medium-high heat. Pour in the bag of steak strips. Move them around to separate them a bit and cook for about 3 minutes on each side, depending on the thickness of meat. The edges should be brown and crispy. Transfer the steak to a bowl and set aside; keep the pan on the stove.

In a medium bowl, whisk together the 2 teaspoons cornstarch, brown sugar, soy sauce, and water. Set aside.

Heat the remaining 2 tablespoons oil in the steak pan over medium heat. Add the scallions, garlic, and ginger and stir for a minute to release flavors. Add the broccoli and stir-fry for 1 to 2 minutes. Add the sauce mixture and beef to pan and let the sauce simmer for 2 to 3 minutes or until the sauce thickens and broccoli softens to desired texture. Add the cashews and stir well.

Plate and serve with jasmine rice. Garnish with additional scallions if desired.

 **notes**

bored-in-the-house gnocchi

complete meal

ready in 1 hour, 30 minutes

serves 4 to 6

3 pounds russet or Yukon
gold potatoes

3 cups all-purpose
flour of choice

1 teaspoon kosher salt

1½ eggs (get the ½ by
whisking one egg and
use half the mixture)

1 (24-ounce) jar marinara
sauce, divided

1 cup grated Parmesan
cheese

Fresh ball mozzarella, sliced

8 to 10 whole basil leaves

+ added yum:

Garnish with *more* fresh
grated Parmesan cheese
and chopped basil

This is a special recipe because the first time we made it was the night the idea of our cookbook was born. Probably just like you, the early "sheltering in place" days of the pandemic had us feeling a little loopy and out of sorts, and—dare I say?—bored. We have always tried to live by the philosophy "only the boring get bored," so that night, after spending too much time on TikTok and the then-ubiquitous "bored in the house" videos, we kicked ourselves in the butts and reminded each other that we're creative and fun girls! We decided to throw a really nice Saturday night dinner party and challenged each other to make something we loved at restaurants but had never made before. We landed on gnocchi. We combined and changed up a few recipes that sounded good and forged ahead.

So those hilarious "bored in the house" TikToks inspired such a fun night (when we were anything but bored), and the name of the recipe. They also inspired us to keep laughing and creating rather than wallowing. That's why this dish is very special to us. It reminds us of how capable we all are of creating our own light and fun during dark times. We hope you'll make this when you need a little self-nurturing or as a reminder to yourself that you are capable of creating your own light!

Fill a large stockpot with water and add the unpeeled potatoes (the skins protect the potatoes from getting waterlogged and mushy). Bring to a boil and simmer for 15 to 20 minutes. You want them to be barely fork tender, no more, no less; they should not be too mushy to grate. Drain the potatoes in a colander and let sit in the colander until cool enough to touch. Peel the potatoes; you should be able to do this fairly easily with just your hands. Rice the potatoes with a potato ricer. (Or a box grater works well. That's what we use!)

Mound the grated potatoes in the middle of a large cutting board or on a very clean, dry countertop. Top with the flour and sprinkle with the salt. Using your hands, create a well in the flour

 **notes**

by scooping out the center of your mound. Drop the eggs into the center of the well and whisk with a fork. Very gradually start pulling the flour to the potato and egg mixture with the fork. Then use your hands to bring all the ingredients together and knead to form dough.

Shape the dough into a large, rectangular block about 4 inches wide and 8 to 10 inches long. Cut the rectangle into 8 to 10 strips of dough 1 to 1½ inches wide. Roll each piece into a long ¾-inch-thick rope by gently pushing with your fingers. Try to make evenly sized ropes. Using a sharp, non-serrated knife or pastry cutter, cut the dough ropes into uniform 1-inch pieces. Roll each gnocchi shape down a gnocchi paddle to create grooves. An egg grater or the back of a fork works, too. You can also forgo the lines! Toss the pieces with a little flour to prevent sticking. For best results, cook the gnocchi right away, or cover with light kitchen towel and cook within an hour.

Preheat the oven to 350°F. Grease a 9 x 13-inch baking dish.

Bring a large pot of water to a boil and add a good pinch of salt. Gently drop in the gnocchi; we recommend using a spider spoon. Cook the gnocchi until they start floating, 2 to 5 minutes. Remove from the water with a spider spoon or strainer and place in a bowl.

Meanwhile, heat up the marinara sauce in a medium saucepan. Spoon a layer of the marinara sauce into the greased baking dish.

In a large bowl, lightly toss together the cooked gnocchi, Parmesan, and all but about ½ cup of the remaining marinara sauce. Add the sauced gnocchi to the baking dish and pour the remaining sauce on top. Top with the mozzarella slices and basil leaves. Bake until the cheese is melted and the sauce is bubbling, about 10 minutes. Scoop, serve, enjoy!

+ added yum: Garnish with more fresh grated Parmesan cheese and chopped basil.

tip

We use gluten-free flour for this recipe too and it's great!

browned butter + sage-dunked sweet potato gnocchi

complete meal

ready in 45 minutes

serves 4

gnocchi

2 pounds sweet potatoes

⅔ cup whole-milk
    ricotta cheese

1 teaspoon freshly ground
    black pepper

1 teaspoon kosher salt

2 cups all-purpose flour
    (gluten-free is OK),
    plus more for desired
    dough consistency

browned butter sauce

½ cup (1 stick) unsalted butter

4 cloves garlic, sliced

½ cup torn sage leaves

1 cup thin ribbons of
    Tuscan kale

1 cup finely grated
    Parmesan cheese

Kosher salt and freshly
    ground black pepper

+ added yum:
    More Parm cheese

This trendy rendition of gnocchi is something we were seeing quite a bit from internet foodies and wanted to come up with our version. We like to add a boost of nutrition wherever we can and this seemed like a perfect opportunity to add some bright green kale to our bodies. This tastes so special, if we owned a restaurant, it would be on the menu every night.

make the gnocchi

Pierce the sweet potatoes all over with a knife. Wrap each in a damp paper towel. Microwave on high until very soft, 12 to 13 minutes. Let sit until cool enough to handle, then peel and discard the skins.

Mash the potatoes in a large bowl until smooth. Stir in the ricotta, pepper, and salt. Distribute the flour into the mixture and mix with a strong fork until a dough forms; it should be loose and not stick to the sides of the bowl. Add more flour a little at a time, if required.

Dust a work surface with flour and begin to work the dough gently with floured hands. Keep folding the dough in half and pressing softly with the heel of your hand, turning the dough often to work all areas. Continue until the dough isn't sticky. Add more flour if needed, but just small increments of sprinkles. You're trying to get rid of the stickiness and just bring it to tender dough. Divide the dough into six equal portions, then roll them into balls.

On a fresh floured surface, roll each ball into a 1-inch-thick, foot-long rope. One rope at a time, cut each crosswise in twelve 1-inch pieces. Roll each gnocchi shape down the gnocchi paddle to create grooves. An egg grater or the back of a fork works, too. You can also forgo the lines!

browned butter +
sage-dunked sweet
potato gnocchi

Bring a large pot of water to a boil and add a good pinch of salt. Drop the gnocchi into the boiling water—a spider strainer or large slotted spoon works great for this. Cook the gnocchi, stirring gently at times so they don't stick to the bottom, for 5 minutes or until most are floating at the top. You want tender, but still firm, gnocchi. Remove from water with a spider spoon or strainer and place in a bowl.

make the sauce

Melt the butter in a large skillet over medium heat and add the garlic. When the butter foam is gone, add the sage and cook until the butter is brown and the sage is crispy, about 3 minutes.

Add all the gnocchi to the skillet. Gently toss to coat with the sauce. Add the kale and toss gently again. Add the Parmesan cheese and season to taste with salt and pepper. Divide into four bowls and serve.

+ added yum: Garnish with more cheese!

tips

- A gnocchi paddle is fun to use and available for as little as $5 online.
- Don't rinse the cooked gnocchi. And to save time and cleanup, use a spider spoon or straining spoon to move them directly from pot to saucepan.
- Plan ahead and have all the sauce ingredients ready to go so you can quickly make the sauce while the gnocchi is cooking.

♡ **notes**

chickpea penne alla vodka

complete meal

ready in 30 minutes

serves 2 to 3

¼ cup extra-virgin olive oil

1 large or 2 small shallots, finely chopped

4 cloves fresh garlic, smashed, peeled, and chopped

½ cup tomato paste

2 tablespoons vodka

1 cup heavy cream

½ teaspoon chili flakes (optional)

8 ounces Banza chickpea penne pasta or other pasta of choice

½ cup grated Parmesan cheese

2 tablespoons unsalted butter

Kosher salt and freshly ground black pepper to taste

+ added yum: Fresh basil, chopped in ribbons, and additional grated Parmesan

Everyone needs a comforting, impressive pasta dish they've mastered that can be whipped up in a jiffy with just a few pantry staples. If you don't have one in your back pocket ... well, you do now! You'll be surprised how easy, tomatoey, creamy, and scrumptious this is. The warm hue of orange is beautiful to your eyes and soul.

Heat the olive oil in a large saucepan or skillet over medium heat. Add the shallots and sauté until just soft. Add the garlic and sauté for about a minute (don't let it burn!). Stir in the tomato paste and cook until it's caramelized, about 5 minutes (it will turn a rich, dark red color). Add the vodka and stir until mostly evaporated, about 2 minutes. Add the cream and chili flakes, stirring well.

Meanwhile, cook the pasta in a large pot of salted, boiling water according to package instructions. Drain, reserving ½ cup of the water for sauce.

Once the cream and chili flakes are incorporated into the sauce, add the reserved pasta water and Parmesan and cook until thickened. Add the drained pasta and stir well to incorporate the sauce and pasta. Add the butter and stir until creamy, then salt and pepper to taste. Transfer the pasta to bowls and serve.

+ added yum: Finish with additional Parmesan cheese and ribbons of fresh basil on top.

tips

- This pasta dish is quick and delicious as a hearty side or as a meatless meal all on its own. If you want to elevate it, add meatballs or sausage.
- You can use any pasta, but the chickpea Banza is a great option for added protein and a gluten-free pasta meal!

lemony risotto with zucchini + asparagus

ready in 1 hour

serves 4 to 5

5 cups chicken broth

3 tablespoons unsalted
butter, divided

1 leek, sliced thin (see Tips)

1 large zucchini, shredded

8 asparagus stalks, bottoms
trimmed and cut into
bite-size pieces

Pinch kosher salt

Freshly ground black pepper

¼ cup olive oil

1 yellow onion, finely chopped

8 sprigs fresh thyme

4 cloves fresh garlic,
smashed, peeled,
and chopped

1½ cups Arborio rice or
medium-grain white
rice, uncooked

½ cup white wine of choice

Grated zest and juice
of 1 lemon

¾ cup grated Parmesan
cheese

+ added yum:

Extra Parmesan cheese
and 4 to 5 leaves fresh
basil for garnish

Risotto is a classic Italian rice dish that is both comforting and quite elegant. This recipe was inspired by Sharon and Kelsey's trip to Italy after Kelsey graduated from law school. We tried to recreate a lemony risotto we had at Sciuè Sciuè, a very cool cucina in Rome. We added asparagus for more veggies and color.

Making risotto is easier than you may think; it just requires patience and stirring, as the rice cooks slowly.

In a medium saucepan, bring the chicken broth to a low simmer, so it stays warm all through the risotto cooking process. (The warm broth helps release the starch, making your risotto creamy and dreamy.)

In a large, heavy-bottomed skillet or saucepan, melt 2 tablespoons of the butter over medium heat. Add the leek, zucchini, and asparagus, and sauté for 5 minutes or until slightly tender. Add a 3-finger pinch of salt and 2 twists/grinds of fresh pepper. Scrape the vegetables into a bowl.

Melt the remaining 1 tablespoon butter in the same pan. Add the oil, onion, thyme, and garlic, and cook for 1 to 2 minutes (don't let the garlic burn). Add the rice and cook, stirring until lightly toasted, about 3 minutes. (This step is important because it adds a nutty elegance.) Add the wine and stir until it's absorbed into the rice.

Still stirring, slowly add about ½ cup of the warm broth and cook and stir until the liquid is absorbed. Continue cooking and stirring, adding additional broth after each pour has been absorbed. It will take 25 to 30 minutes to use up all of the broth and for the risotto to become creamy and al dente. Stir in the reserved veggies and lemon zest and juice. Finish with the Parmesan, stirring well.

+ added yum: Garnish with fresh basil and more cheese!

tips

- To slice the leek, use a sharp chef's knife to cut off the root and rough green top of the leek, then slice in half lengthwise. Place the cut sides down and slice thinly into half-moon shapes. Throw in a colander and rinse off any dirt.
- We toss whole sprigs of thyme in then remove the branches when the leaves have fallen off into the rice.
- The rice will stop drinking when it's done. It should have just a little bite to the texture—a slightly al dente feel.

Kelsey and Sharon walking the beautiful streets of Rome on their way to Sciuè Sciuè.

creamy risotto with chicken sausage + pancetta

complete meal

ready in 1 hour, 15 minutes

serves 4 to 5

5 cups chicken broth

2 tablespoons
    unsalted butter

4 or 5 links chicken Parmesan
    Italian sausage

5 ounces pancetta, chopped

1 yellow onion, finely chopped

1 red bell pepper, cored,
    seeded, and chopped

4 cloves fresh garlic,
    smashed, peeled,
    and chopped

⅔ cup coarsely chopped
    mushrooms of choice

1½ cups Arborio or medium-
    grain white rice, uncooked

¾ cup white wine of choice

¾ cup freshly grated
    Parmesan cheese

+ added yum:

    1 tablespoon chopped
    fresh basil and extra
    Parmesan cheese

 **notes**

We love this recipe because it feels like a cozy, inviting ristorante in Rome. Kelsey and Sharon were so inspired by their trip to Italy that we have a couple of risotto recipes in this book. We've learned it's as comforting as a bowl of pasta and fun to change the rice's personality by using seasonal ingredients, different kinds of meats and cheeses, and mixing up red or white wines.

Bring the broth to a simmer in a medium saucepan. (Simmering the broth keeps it warm through the cooking process, which helps release the starch in the rice and makes your risotto creamy and dreamy.)

In a large, heavy-bottomed skillet or sauté pan, melt the butter over medium heat. Add the sausage and brown until cooked through. Remove and set aside.

Add the pancetta to the now-empty pan and sauté until golden brown, about 5 minutes. Add the onions, bell pepper, garlic, and mushrooms, and sauté, scraping up the browned bits on the bottom of the pan or until tender, about 5 minutes.

Add the rice to the pan, stir to coat, and toast for about 2 minutes. (This step is important because it adds a nutty elegance.) Add the wine and simmer until the wine has almost been completely absorbed by the rice, about 1 minute. Still stirring, slowly add about ½ cup of the warm broth and cook and stir until the liquid is absorbed. Continue cooking and stirring, adding additional broth after each pour has been absorbed. It will take 25 to 30 minutes to use up all of the broth and for the risotto to become creamy and al dente.

Meanwhile, slice the sausage and keep warm.

Stir the Parmesan cheese into the risotto and transfer to a serving platter or individual bowls, topping with the sliced sausage.

+ added yum: Garnish with *more* fresh grated Parmesan cheese and chopped basil.

fast + fab brown sugar-buttered salmon

ready in 20 minutes

serves 4

2 cloves fresh garlic,
    smashed, peeled,
    and chopped

1 cup (½ stick) unsalted butter

4 (5- to 6-ounce) center-
    cut salmon fillets,
    skin on or off

1 large lemon, cut in half

¼ cup packed brown sugar

Kosher salt and freshly
    ground black
    pepper to taste

 **notes**

Salmon is filled with omega-3 fatty acids known for reducing inflammation and improving heart and brain health. Many shy away from making it because it seems intimidating. But our salmon is super simple, scrumptious, and turns anyone who tries it into a salmon lover. Bet this becomes a regular on your dinner rotation—it is on all of ours!

Preheat the oven to 400°F. Line a baking sheet with foil.

Place the garlic and butter in a medium glass bowl and microwave for 1 minute to melt the butter. Let sit for 2 minutes to allow the garlic to infuse the butter.

Arrange the salmon on the prepared sheet and pat with a paper towel to remove any excess moisture. Squeeze one lemon half over salmon.

Stir the brown sugar into the melted butter and pour half the mixture into a separate bowl. Brush the salmon with the remaining brown sugar mixture.

Bake the salmon until it is cooked to desired doneness. (The FDA says most seafood should be cooked to an internal temperature of 145°F. Many foodies and chefs say fish tastes best somewhere between 120°F and 145°F. We bake salmon for 12 to 15 minutes and probably end up somewhere in the middle.) Remove the salmon from the oven and brush with the remaining brown sugar mixture. Squeeze the other half of the lemon over the tops, season with salt and pepper to taste, and serve.

good ole chicken + waffles

ready in 1 hour
(+ 8 hours marinating)
serves 4

2 cups buttermilk
1 tablespoon Frank's
RedHot hot sauce
2 shallots, sliced thin
4 cloves fresh garlic,
smashed, peeled,
and chopped
1 teaspoon kosher salt,
plus more to taste
1 teaspoon freshly ground
black pepper, plus
more to taste
4 (small to medium) boneless,
skinless chicken breasts
3½ cups all-purpose
flour of choice
3½ teaspoons baking powder
2 teaspoons paprika
½ teaspoon garlic powder
½ teaspoon red
pepper flakes
Kosher salt and freshly
ground black
pepper to taste
Canola oil for frying
Waffle mix of choice (we like
Bob's Red Mill or King
Arthur), cooked according
to package instructions

+ added yum:
Powdered sugar and
good maple syrup

We had a favorite restaurant in Portland that made the best chicken and waffles. When it went out of business, we just had to figure out how to make them at home. It took a few attempts, but we think we nailed it. Such a fun meal to eat!

In a medium bowl, whisk together the buttermilk, hot sauce, shallots, garlic, salt, and pepper. Set marinade aside.

Cover with parchment paper and use a meat mallet to pound chicken breasts until each is about ½ inch thick. Transfer to a bowl, add the marinade, and turn the chicken to thoroughly coat. Cover the bowl with a lid or plastic wrap and marinate in the refrigerator for at least 8 hours, but no more than 24 hours.

Preheat the oven to 300°F.

When ready to cook the chicken, mix the flour, baking powder, paprika, garlic powder, red pepper flakes, and salt and pepper to taste in a medium bowl. Using tongs, remove a piece of chicken from the marinade and dredge it in the flour mixture, then return it for another dip in the marinade, then another dredge in the flour mixture. Lay on a large plate. Repeat to coat all the pieces of chicken.

Pour at least 3 inches oil into a Dutch oven or another large frying pot. Heat over medium-high heat until it reaches 350°F on a candy or deep-fry thermometer. Carefully lower two of the chicken breasts into the oil. We like using a spider spatula to prevent splashing. Fry for 2½ minutes, then flip the chicken over, and fry for another 2½ minutes or until the chicken is cooked through and the internal temperature reaches 165°F on an instant-read thermometer. Remove the chicken from oil and place on a baking sheet lined with paper towels to absorb excess oil. Then, place chicken on a wire rack on a sheet pan and put in the oven to keep warm. Repeat with the remaining chicken.

To serve, place a waffle on each plate and top with fried chicken breast.

 **notes**

+ added yum: Sprinkle a little powdered sugar and pour maple syrup over the top.

tips

- Use gluten-free flour for a crispier crunch!
- Be sure to check that you have all the ingredients for your waffle mix.
- Frying deserves your full attention for safety. Put someone else on waffle duty.

greece-inspired buttery pan-seared scallops with pea puree

ready in 35 minutes

serves 3 to 4

12 to 16 sea scallops

All-purpose flour

Kosher salt and freshly
    ground black
    pepper to taste

3 tablespoons unsalted
    butter, divided

1½ tablespoons
    extra-virgin olive oil

2 cloves fresh garlic,
    smashed, peeled,
    and chopped

2 tablespoons chopped
    fresh parsley

1 fresh small lemon,
    cut into wedges

Pea Puree (recipe follows)

When Kendall and Sharon visited Greece, they found scallops and pea purees on most every menu. It became one of their favorite dishes, whether they shared it as an appetizer or made it their main meal. When they got home, they were determined to recreate the dish. It immediately transports us all to Greece's lovely islands! Bonus: Scallops are a beautiful, lean protein packed with vitamin B12!

Remove the small side muscle from the scallops and rinse with cold water in a strainer. Drain and gently pat each scallop dry with paper towels.

Sprinkle about ½ cup flour on a plate or baking sheet large enough to fit all the scallops. Lay each scallop on the floured surface and flip to lightly coat each side. Season with salt and pepper on both sides.

In a large skillet, heat 2 tablespoons of the butter and the oil over medium-high heat. When the pan is hot (the oil and butter look shimmery), place the scallops in the hot oil. Begin at the top of the pan and set them in gently, moving clockwise. Cook undisturbed until golden on the bottom and opaque on top, 2 to 3 minutes, depending on the size of scallops. When ready, flip them over in the same order you laid them down. (This helps them cook evenly.) Cook the scallops 1 to 2 minutes more or until completely opaque. Transfer to a plate or platter in the same order you placed the scallops in the pan.

Reduce the heat under the pan to medium. Add the remaining 1 tablespoon butter and the garlic. Then the parsley. Cook until the garlic is softened and remove the pan from the heat.

Spoon the pea puree (next page) onto serving plates and then smear with a creative swoosh. Top with scallops and spoon the garlic butter over each. Give a squeeze of fresh lemon and serve.

tip

Try scattering additional fresh peas on the puree and serve with Roasted Fingerling Potatoes + Fennel + Parm (page 154).

pea purée

ready in 15 minutes
serves 4

This plant-based protein puree is a great source of vitamins C and E. It's scrumptious under these scallops, or any fish or meat.

2 tablespoons unsalted butter
1 shallot, finely chopped
2 cloves fresh garlic, smashed,
    peeled, and chopped
2 cups frozen peas
¼ cup chicken broth
¼ cup ricotta cheese
¼ cup chopped fresh parsley
Fresh lemon juice to taste
Kosher salt and freshly
    ground black pepper

+ added yum:
    fresh peas, chives,
    and arugula

Melt the butter in a medium saucepan over medium-high heat. Add the shallot and sauté until soft and clear. Add the garlic and sauté until softened, about 1 minute. Add the peas and broth and cook until all the ingredients are combined and the peas are soft—not mushy—2 to 3 minutes. Be careful not to overcook the peas.

Pour the mixture into a high-speed blender or food processor. Add the ricotta, parsley, and a squeeze of lemon and blend until smooth. Add salt and pepper to taste.

If necessary, reheat the puree when ready to serve. You can create a bed of the puree with a knife or spoon, or you can put it in a pastry bag and swirl on the plates.

+ added yum: Use fresh peas, chives, and arugula as garnishes on your plate or platter.

hazelnut-crusted fish, just for the halibut

ready in 25 minutes

serves 4

⅔ cup hazelnuts

2 teaspoons minced
   fresh thyme

½ teaspoon freshly
   ground black pepper

1 egg white

4 (5- to 6-ounce)
   halibut fillets

2 tablespoons
   unsalted butter

2 teaspoons extra-virgin
   olive oil

4 orange wedges

 **notes**

Not only is halibut delicious, it's high in magnesium. Our hearts and bones love that! And we love that it doesn't have an overly fishy taste; that's why it's one of our favorites. Grilled or baked halibut is always wonderful, but sometimes it's nice to dress it up a bit. Our hazelnut crust with fresh thyme is quite special but doesn't overwhelm the simple freshness of the fish. A squirt of orange just before serving makes it even better. We serve it over our Creamy Coconut Lentils + Veggie Friends (page 137) for even more decadence.

Combine the hazelnuts, thyme, and pepper in a gallon-size resealable plastic bag. Seal the bag and coarsely crush the nuts with a meat mallet or rolling pin. Shake the bag to mix all the ingredients. Spread on a plate, dividing into four areas for each piece of fish. This helps ensure equal coating on each piece.

Beat the egg white in a small glass bowl. Brush both sides of the fish fillets with egg, then dredge each in the nut mixture, coating all over. You may have some mixture left. Place the fillets on a parchment paper-lined plate and press the nut mixture into the fish to be sure it all adheres.

Heat the butter and oil in a large sauté pan over medium heat. Place the fish in the pan and cook for 4 to 5 minutes on each side or until the nuts are toasted and the fish flakes easily when poked with a fork. (Fish should reach an internal temperature of 145°F.)

Serve with orange wedges and squeeze a bit over the fish just before eating.

pork chops for the applesauce

ready in 50 minutes

serves 4

4 (1- to 2-inch-thick) bone-in
porterhouse pork chops

Onion powder to taste

Kosher salt and freshly
ground black
pepper to taste

¼ cup vegetable oil

6 tablespoons
unsalted butter

4 to 5 cloves fresh garlic,
smashed, peeled,
and chopped

Chopped fresh sage

Chopped fresh parsley

Leaves from 3 sprigs
fresh thyme

¼ teaspoon red
pepper flakes

6 tablespoons packed
dark brown sugar

 notes

Pork chops and applesauce—a nostalgic combination for me. The duo has always made me feel safe, and I wanted to share that with my kids. I tried to cook the perfect pork chop for many years, but with. I tried many recipes and various techniques, but it often felt like the meat was being steamed, leaving the chops rubbery. One day, I decided to keep it simple and just keep moisture away from the chops, cooking them in a skillet. The result was a juicy, perfectly textured pork chop. I learned they don't need a lot of fuss, just attention to a few small details. Don't forget to serve with our Applesauce (page 166).

—Sharon

Pat the chops very dry with a paper towel. Coat each side with onion powder, salt, and pepper based on your taste preferences. Let sit at room temperature for 30 minutes. If you see more moisture escape after seasoning, gently pat dry again, trying not to remove seasoning. Add more seasoning if needed.

Heat the oil in a stainless steel or cast iron skillet over medium-high heat. When the oil starts to shimmer, add the pork chops and cook on one side for only 1 minute. Turn the chops and cook another minute. Continue to cook, flipping every minute, for 8 to 10 minutes. (Turning the chops every minute prevents the them from curling up and allows them to cook evenly.) Pull the pork chops out of the pan when their internal temperature reaches 140°F. Set aside.

Reduce the heat under the skillet to low. Add the butter, garlic, sage, parsley, thyme, and red pepper flakes, stirring constantly to infuse the flavors into butter. Add the brown sugar, stirring until well blended and simmer for about 2 minutes. Return the chops to the pan and spoon the herb butter over the tops. Remove the pork chops from pan when their internal temperature reaches 145°F.

Let the pork rest for about 5 minutes. Pour any remaining mixture from the pan on top of pork chops before serving.

tip

Thoroughly dry pork chops before cooking. Getting them bone dry is the key to juicy, delicious pork chops.

sexy slow cooker barbacoa beef

prep is 15 minutes
ready in 6 to 8 hours on low
serves 4 to 6

1 small yellow onion,
   finely chopped
6 cloves fresh garlic,
   smashed, peeled,
   and chopped
1 (4-ounce) can mild
   diced green chilis
3 tablespoons tomato paste
1 tablespoon dried
   Mexican oregano
1 tablespoon chili powder
1 tablespoon ground cumin
½ teaspoon paprika
¼ teaspoon ground clove
3 bay leaves
1½ cups beef broth
¼ cup fresh lime juice
2 tablespoons apple
   cider vinegar
2 tablespoons extra-virgin
   olive oil
Kosher salt and freshly
   ground black pepper
3 pounds chuck roast
   or beef brisket

We love barbacoa beef, but some in our family are not super spicy food enthusiasts. Barbacoa is traditionally roasted low and slow over an open flame with chipotle chilis in adobo. We bring you the personality of barbacoa with the ease of a slow cooker and without the heat. The yummy beef is perfect for tacos, burritos, nachos, quesadillas, enchiladas, served over rice, or in salads. Make extra and freeze it! These ingredients + sexy slow cooker = the easy, authentic feel of this Spanish and Caribbean classic style of beef.

Turn the slow cooker on low. Whisk all the ingredients except the meat together in the cooker. Cut several slits in the meat with a sharp paring knife. Add to the slow cooker. Cover and cook for 6 to 8 hours. Pull the meat apart using forks and serve.

 **notes**

sexy slow cooker shoyu hawaiian chicken

prep is 15 minutes

ready in 8 hours on low
   (4 to 5 hours on high)

serves 6 to 8

1½ cups soy sauce

1½ cups water

2 tablespoons
   Worcestershire sauce

1 tablespoon rice
   wine vinegar

1 cup granulated sugar

½ cup packed brown sugar

2-inch piece fresh ginger,
   peeled and grated

8 cloves fresh garlic,
   smashed, peeled,
   and chopped

⅛ teaspoon red
   pepper flakes

5 tablespoons cornstarch

3 pounds (12 thighs) boneless
   skinless chicken thighs

+ added yum:
   Sliced scallions for garnish

This recipe was born from our love of a local Hawaiian BBQ restaurant. We aren't going to stop going there to get it, but we do love to guess the flavors and recreate dishes at home that we enjoy. We also really love great slow cooker recipes that can cook all day so we have a favorite at our fingertips. Serve with rice and a green salad with pineapple and citrus.

Turn the slow cooker on low. Combine the soy sauce, water, Worcestershire, vinegar, granulated sugar, brown sugar, ginger, garlic, and red pepper flakes in the cooker. Whisk in the cornstarch until dissolved completely. Add the chicken thighs and cook for 8 hours on low (or for 4 to 5 hours on high).

+ added yum: Garnish with sliced scallions.

tip

The shredded chicken also makes for great sandwiches on Hawaiian rolls.

♡ notes

sexy slow cooker warm-spiced kidney bean curry

prep is 15 minutes
ready in 5 to 6 hours on low
serves 4 to 5

2 tablespoons avocado oil

1 tablespoon cumin seeds

2 teaspoons curry powder

1 teaspoon roasted coriander

1 teaspoon turmeric

½ teaspoon cardamom

Freshly ground black pepper

1 large red onion, chopped
    fine (2 cups)

3 cloves fresh garlic,
    smashed, peeled,
    and chopped

3 (15.5-ounce) cans kidney
    beans, not drained

1 (28-ounce) can diced
    tomatoes

+ added yum:
    Fresh chopped cilantro
    and buttered jasmine rice

We love recipes that our friend, the sexy slow cooker, can cook for us while we work. We also love recipes that don't require a lot of prep and dirty pans. The slow cook of this curry makes a gorgeous, fragrant, warm-spiced bean dish. The kidney beans keep their texture well and make for a very hearty, meatless meal packed with plant-based protein. The warm spices will make your home smell so cozy and inviting.

Turn the slow cooker on low. Combine the oil and cumin seeds in the cooker and let them cook gently while you gather and prep everything else. Add the curry powder, coriander, turmeric, cardamom, and ground pepper to the cooker. Whisk well and let the spices infuse the oil while you chop the onion and garlic cloves. Add the onion, garlic, beans, and tomatoes to the spice and oil mixture. Stir well and put on the lid. Cook on low for 5 to 6 hours.

+ added yum: Sprinkle with cilantro and serve with buttered jasmine rice.

 **notes**

shrimp + grits

ready in 30 minutes

serves 4

4 slices bacon, chopped

1½ pounds medium shrimp, peeled and deveined

2 tablespoons unsalted butter

1 medium red bell pepper, cored, seeded, and diced

1 medium orange bell pepper, cored, seeded, and diced

1 medium red onion, finely chopped (about 1 cup)

4 scallions (white and green parts), sliced thin

3 cloves fresh garlic, smashed, peeled, and chopped

Juice of 1 small lemon

¼ cup cornstarch

2 tablespoons Old Bay seasoning

1 tablespoon paprika

1 cup chicken broth

Creamy, Dreamy, Cheesy Polenta (page 149), using 2 cups shredded sharp cheddar cheese instead of Parmesan

Chopped fresh parsley and thinly sliced scallion greens for garnish

Southern-style shrimp and grits is down-home comfort that is perfect for a family dinner and special enough for company! We use Old Bay as our not-so-secret seasoning. If you've used it, you know exactly why it's perfect in this recipe. The smell of the spices will elicit some of your favorite coastal memories. For a modern twist, we use our creamy polenta (page 149) rather than traditional white grits.

In a large skillet, fry the bacon over medium heat until crispy. Remove with a slotted spoon and set aside in a medium bowl. Sauté the shrimp in the bacon grease until pink, about 5 minutes a batch. Remove cooked shrimp and set aside in the bowl with the bacon.

Melt the butter in bacon grease. Add the bell peppers, onion, scallions, and garlic, and sauté for 3 minutes or until tender. Squeeze lemon juice over everything and stir, making sure to scrape the pan to loosen any crispy bits stuck to the bottom. Add the cornstarch, Old Bay, and paprika and cook, stirring well or until everything begins to brown, 1 to 2 minutes. Add the broth and stir well. Let simmer for 10 minutes or until the sauce has thickened. Remove from heat. Stir the shrimp and bacon into the vegetables until everything is incorporated.

Spoon the polenta into a bowl, top with the shrimp mixture, and garnish with fresh parsley and scallions. Serve immediately to keep the polenta creamy!

 **notes**

tips

- Here's our game plan for getting the shrimp and grits done at the same time: Start the polenta when you fry the bacon, then stir them occasionally while cooking the shrimp and veggies, keeping an eye on them the entire time. After sautéing the veggies, finish the polenta by adding the butter, cream, and cheddar cheese and stirring until creamy. If needed, reheat the shrimp mixture.
- Newbie cooks might want to make the shrimp mixture first so you can concentrate on it and not be distracted by making the polenta. It won't hurt the dish to quickly heat the shrimp mixture when you are ready to serve it.
- For a weeknight dinner, we reduce the butter by half and skip the cream when making the polenta. When making it for company, we go all in to elevate it and make it extra scrumptious!

turkey + sweet potato + kale bowls

complete meal

ready in 30 minutes
serves 3 to 4

3 tablespoons extra-virgin
    olive oil
1 pound ground turkey
⅔ cup finely chopped
    red onion
⅔ cup chopped yellow and/
    or orange bell peppers
4 cloves fresh garlic,
    smashed, peeled,
    and chopped
2 cups cubed, peeled sweet
    potatoes (2 large or
    3 medium sweet potatoes)
1 tablespoon cinnamon sugar
1 heaping tablespoon finely
    chopped fresh sage
1 teaspoon fresh
    thyme leaves
1 tablespoon chili powder
½ teaspoon ground cumin
¼ teaspoon garlic powder
¼ teaspoon onion powder
Freshly ground black pepper
2 cups chopped ribbed
    fresh Tuscan kale
Chopped fresh parsley
    for garnish
+ added yum:
    Shredded Gruyère or
    mozzarella cheese to top

This is one of those recipes that seems like no big deal at first glance, but we're pretty confident it will quickly become a family favorite. It's like a reconstructed hamburger and potato casserole, but with a flavor and nutrition boost. The cinnamon and chili undertones are a delightfully warm surprise. We love power bowl food! It's so comforting and simple after a long day.

In a Dutch oven, heat the olive oil over medium-high heat. Add the ground turkey and cook until almost brown. Add the onion, peppers, and garlic. Cook until the onions are soft, 2 to 3 minutes.

Add the sweet potatoes, cinnamon sugar, sage, thyme, chili powder, cumin, garlic powder, onion powder, and ground pepper to taste. Incorporate well. Cover the Dutch oven and cook over medium heat, stirring occasionally or until the sweet potatoes are soft but not mushy, 15 to 20 minutes. Add the kale and stir until tender, about 1 minute. Garnish with fresh parsley and serve.

+ added yum: Before garnishing with parsley, top the sweet potato mixture with shredded Gruyère or mozzarella cheese and heat in a 400°F oven to melt the cheese. Keep an eye on the cheese and remove as soon as it melts.

tip

This is one of those recipes that is delicious even if you don't have every single ingredient, but if you do, it's extra magical!

 **notes**

fun nights
with friends

The dinner table is where hearts are tied together. Cooking food for friends is a beautiful way to develop and strengthen important and meaningful bonds. Taking time to think about what foods your friends enjoy, shopping for them, cleaning the house, and setting a beautiful table are all acts of respect and love. It shows friends that they are important to you.

We have always loved a kitchen or backyard filled with friends, and over the years, we have developed some special traditions. We have some beautiful recipes and entertaining ideas that we hope inspire some beautiful and fun nights with your friends. Whether you're a well-established entertainer or just starting out, our recipes are perfect for entertaining!

sweetie beetie risotto with goat cheese

ready in 1 hour, 15 minutes
serves 4 to 5

5 cups chicken broth

3 tablespoons
unsalted butter

¼ cup extra-virgin olive oil

1 yellow onion, finely
chopped (about 1 cup)

½ teaspoon minced
fresh thyme

4 cloves fresh garlic,
smashed, peeled,
and chopped

1½ cups Arborio rice or
medium-grain white rice

½ cup red wine of choice

2 raw medium red beets,
stemmed, peeled,
and shredded (with
a box grater)

Grated zest and juice
of ½ lemon

⅓ cup goat cheese

½ cup freshly grated
Parmesan cheese

5 leaves fresh basil
for garnish

This risotto has become a fun, celebratory dish in the Peddie house. The gorgeous, deep red color from the beets makes this a festive meal for Valentines, Galentines, or a couples' dinner party. It also makes a brilliant side to a Christmas meal.

The earthiness of the beets combined with the creamy smoothness of goat cheese makes a balanced, decadent combination. The color is rich and natural and sets a loving tone for a heartfelt meal. This recipe turns beet skeptics into beet lovers.

Bring the broth to a simmer in a medium saucepan. (Simmering the broth keeps it warm all through the cooking process, which helps release the starch in the rice and makes your risotto creamy and dreamy.)

In a large, heavy-bottomed skillet or sauté pan, heat the butter and olive oil over medium heat. Add the onion and thyme and sauté until the onion is lightly browned and translucent. Add the garlic and cook for about 1 more minute.

Add the rice and cook until slightly toasted, about 3 minutes. (This adds a nutty elegance to the rice's flavor.) Add the wine and stir until it has almost been completely absorbed by the rice. Still stirring, slowly add about ½ cup of the warm broth and cook and stir until the liquid is absorbed. Continue cooking and stirring, adding additional broth after each addition has been absorbed. It will take 25 to 30 minutes to use up all of the broth and for the risotto to become creamy and al dente. When the final ½ cup broth has nearly been absorbed, add the beets, stirring them in well. Add lemon zest and juice, then the goat cheese and Parmesan cheese. Stir well.

Garnish with fresh basil and serve!

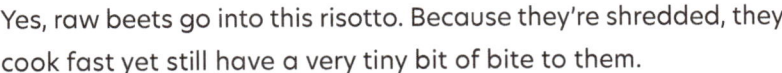

tip

Yes, raw beets go into this risotto. Because they're shredded, they cook fast yet still have a very tiny bit of bite to them.

variation

yellow sweetie beetie risotto

By subbing yellow beets for red beets, you can have another incredible risotto recipe that takes on a slightly sweeter personality and brings a whole different creative vibe. And because of the sweeter, milder taste of the yellow beets, use all Parmesan cheese instead of goat cheese, and white wine instead of red. For a further twist, add 5 ounces of chopped pancetta with the onion.

 **notes**

balsamic-glazed veggie meatloaf

ready in 1 hour, 30 minutes
serves 4 to 6

6 cloves fresh garlic,
    smashed and peeled
1 teaspoon kosher salt,
    plus more to taste
1 cup ketchup, divided
¼ cup plus 2 tablespoons
    balsamic vinegar, divided
3 tablespoons extra-virgin
    olive oil
1 large zucchini, finely
    chopped
1 red bell pepper, cored,
    seeded, and finely chopped
1 orange bell pepper, cored,
    seeded, and finely chopped
1 yellow pepper, cored,
    seeded, finely chopped
2 shallots, finely chopped
⅛ teaspoon red pepper flakes
Freshly ground black pepper
2 large eggs, beaten
2 tablespoons finely
    chopped fresh parsley
1 tablespoon finely chopped
    fresh oregano
1 tablespoon fresh
    thyme leaves
½ pound ground pork
1½ pounds ground beef chuck
1 cup panko breadcrumbs
    (GF panko is fine)
¾ cup grated Pecorino
    Romano or Parmesan
    cheese

Having special friends over for dinner means cooking something special. And in our opinion, comfort food done really well is about as special as you can get. This meatloaf contains lots of fresh veggies to enhance its nutrition, flavor, and appearance so your friends will know how much you care! (Serve with your favorite mashed potatoes, or use our Russet + Sweet Potato Mashup recipe on page 162.)

Preheat the oven to 400°F. Line a baking sheet with parchment paper.

Make a garlic paste by chopping the garlic cloves as small as possible. Add 1 teaspoon salt and keep on chopping and combining the salt and garlic together until they form a paste. Set aside to add to the "meat" mixture.

In a small bowl, mix ½ cup of ketchup and 2 tablespoons of balsamic vinegar. Set aside. In another small bowl, mix the remaining ½ cup ketchup and remaining ¼ cup balsamic vinegar. Set aside to create a glaze.

Heat the oil in a large sauté pan over medium-high heat. Add the zucchini, all the peppers, the shallots, red pepper flakes, and salt and pepper to taste. Sauté until almost soft, 4 to 5 minutes. Set aside to cool.

Whisk together the eggs, parsley, oregano, and thyme in a large bowl or stand mixer. Add the garlic paste and the first reserved ketchup mixture, along with the pork, beef, bread crumbs, and grated cheese. Combine well. Add the cooled veggies and combine everything well again.

Mold the meatloaf mixture into a loaf on the lined baking sheet. Bake for 25 minutes. Pour the remaining ketchup mixture over the top of the meatloaf. Bake for another 20 minutes or until the meat registers 160°F on an instant-read thermometer. Allow the meatloaf to rest about 10 minutes before serving.

tip

Sometimes, we shape the meat mixture in a pie dish and bake until the meat registers 160°F (cooking time is sometimes a bit shorter in this shape). Then we add mashed potatoes on top. If you'd like, sprinkle some shredded cheddar cheese on top of the potatoes and broil the pie until the cheese melts. Cut into pie wedges; it makes for another fun presentation. Perfect for family night or an intimate dinner party.

As we've mentioned, GF panko can be substituted anywhere you see panko in our recipes.

big game gumbo

complete meal

ready in 2 hours, 30 minutes
serves 6 to 8

roux

1 heaping cup all-purpose
flour of choice
⅔ cup vegetable oil

gumbo

1 (12-ounce) package
andouille sausages
6 to 8 cups chicken broth
1 bunch celery and
leaves, chopped
1 green bell pepper, cored,
peeled, and diced
1 large yellow onion, diced
1 bunch scallions (white and
green parts), finely chopped
6 cloves garlic, smashed,
peeled, and finely chopped
Leaves from 1 bunch fresh
parsley, finely chopped
(save some for garnish)
½ teaspoon dried thyme
2 tablespoon tomato paste
1 teaspoon gumbo filé
4 pre-baked chicken breasts
1 pound shelled medium
shrimp, cooked
1 teaspoon Cajun seasoning
Cooked white rice for
complete meal serving

Because gumbo is such a popular New Orleans dish, it brings us a celebratory, fun, and festive feeling every time we eat it! And it's great for having the gang over for the game because who wants to be in the kitchen making food once the big game starts? Yes, making a roux is patient work, but if you make the roux and finish the gumbo (and rice) ahead of time, you'll be ready to watch the game with your friends. In fact, it's better for gumbo to sit awhile, as it gets tastier with time. Just heat it up when ready to serve.

make the roux

Combine the flour and oil in a large stockpot and cook over medium-low heat for 30 to 45 minutes, stirring constantly to prevent burning. This takes patience. Cook until you reach a very dark, thick, and gooey consistency. Shut off the heat and set the pot aside.

make the gumbo

In a separate skillet over medium-high heat, brown the sausages, rotating them every 2 minutes until all sides are brown, 5 to 7 minutes. Transfer to a cutting board, and once cool, slice into diagonal coins/discs.

Deglaze the sausage pan by adding ½ cup of the broth and stirring and scraping with a wooden spoon to dislodge all the browned bits. Scrape the broth and drippings into the stockpot with the roux, then add 6 cups of the broth, the celery, bell pepper, onion, scallions, garlic, parsley, thyme, tomato paste, and gumbo filé. Stir well and bring to a boil. Allow to boil, skimming any foam from the top of the pot for 5 to 7 minutes or until the flavors come together.

Add the reserved sausage, along with the chicken, shrimp, and Cajun seasoning. Turn the heat down to low and simmer for another 5 to 10 minutes so everything can warm through and combine. Keep a watchful eye to prevent burning. Allow the gumbo to sit covered for at least 30 minutes.

Reheat immediately before serving. Add more broth for desired consistency and taste to see if it needs more Cajun seasoning. Garnish with parsley and serve over mounds of rice!

braised chicken + hominy

complete meal

ready in 1 hour, 30 minutes

serves 4

4 to 5 radishes, sliced
    into thin rounds
1 red onion, sliced thin
1 medium lime, halved
Up to ½ cup chopped
    fresh cilantro, plus
    more for garnish
Kosher salt and freshly
    ground black
    pepper to taste
8 chicken thighs (with or
    without bones and skin)
1 teaspoon ground cumin
1 teaspoon garlic powder
2 tablespoons extra-virgin
    olive oil, plus more
    as needed
1 yellow onion, chopped
4 to 5 garlic cloves, smashed,
    peeled and chopped
1½ pounds (about 12)
    tomatillos, papery
    husks removed, rinsed
    and quartered
1 (4-ounce) can Hatch green
    chiles, half drained
4 cups (1-quart carton)
    chicken broth
1 (30-ounce) can hominy,
    drained and rinsed
Corn tortillas

These chicken thighs are braised on the stovetop with tomatillos, creating a tangy broth and tender braised meat in a short amount of time. Adding hominy creates a light stew that is amazing on its own, however, we love serving it with crispy corn tortillas for dipping. The lime, red onions, and radishes brighten everything with a scrumptious crunch. Kelsey often entertains with this recipe for a fun and casual night with friends. The meal is warm and nurturing but also has a party vibe.

Combine the radishes and sliced red onion in a bowl and squeeze both lime halves over the vegetables. Add cilantro to taste and toss everything together. Season with salt and pepper. Set aside.

Place the chicken thighs on a plate and coat each side with salt, pepper, cumin, and garlic powder. Heat the olive oil in a large cast iron Dutch oven (or similarly large braising pot). Add the thighs, skin (or skinned) side down, and cook until the skin is crispy (or the meat is lightly browned), 8 to 10 minutes. The thighs will start to raise off the pan a bit when they are ready if left alone until that time. Flip the chicken over and finish cooking, another 5 to 6 minutes. Using tongs, carefully transfer the chicken to a plate or wood cutting board.

Add a bit more olive oil to the pot, and scrape all the brown bits off the bottom. Add the chopped yellow onion and garlic and sauté until the onion begins to soften. Add the tomatillos and salt and pepper to taste. Sauté for 5 to 6 minutes or until the tomatillos just start to get soft. Add the chiles and pour in the broth. Bring to a simmer. Return the chicken to the pot. (If you're using chicken with skin, put the thighs in skin side up.) Reduce the heat a bit and allow the tomatillos to reduce, 20 to 25 minutes.

Add the hominy to the pot and cook until the flavors meld and the sauce thickens enough to cling to your spoon, 20 to 25 minutes. Garnish with additional cilantro.

Toast the tortillas over a gas flame or in a very hot pan on the stove. Serve the tortillas with the radish mixture and chicken and have guests assemble their own; everyone has a different way of enjoying this dish.

tip

Kelsey loves this recipe for entertaining because it's simple but makes an impressive statement. While it seems like it takes a long time, it is pretty hands-off. Once you do the initial chopping, you can mostly leave the pot alone to braise.

 **notes**

burger board inspo

ready in 45 minutes
   (more if serving with
   Oven-Baked Sweet
   Potato Fries)
serves 8

 **notes**

This burger board proves it's all about quality ingredients and the presentation! You know how nice jeans and a quality T-shirt presented with the right jacket and shoes will work just about anywhere on a night out with friends? Our burger and fries board fits that same philosophy. Have your friends over for burgers and fries but serve them on a pretty board using high-quality, simple, and classic ingredients! This is a fun and easy meal that makes your friends feel both relaxed and special.

- Choose a good 80/20 ground chuck from the butcher and form 1-inch-thick patties. Figure about a quarter to a third pound per person. Make them a little bigger than the size of the bun you're going to use.
- Choose good cheese from the deli to top the burger. We love a nice Swiss.
- Veggie toppings: We go for grilled mushrooms and grilled onions. We also like to top our burgers with fresh arugula tossed with a little olive oil and balsamic glaze. You can get creative here with your favorites.
- Choose great buns. Brioche buns are buttery and delicious.
- Consider serving with our Oven-Baked Sweet Potato Fries (page 178). (Prep the potatoes before your friends arrive, then just pop the fries in the oven right before you begin cooking the burgers.)
- Engage your friends around the grill as you throw on the burgers, veggies, and buns. If you can't grill everything simultaneously, grill veggies, then buns, then burgers.
- As everything finishes up cooking, build your beautiful burger board! *Yummm!*

come on over to my pad thai

complete meal

ready in 1 hour
serves 4 to 5

sauce

3 tablespoons packed
   dark brown sugar
2 tablespoons tamarind juice
2 tablespoons fish sauce
2 teaspoons sriracha

chicken

3 large skinless, boneless
   chicken breasts, cut
   into bite-size pieces
1 teaspoon garlic powder
1 teaspoon onion powder
1 teaspoon kosher salt
½ teaspoon freshly
   ground black pepper
¼ cup plus 3 tablespoons
   canola oil, divided
16 ounces pad Thai
   brown rice noodles
4 eggs, beaten
1 lime, cut into wedges
+ added yum
   toppings: mung bean
   sprouts, cashews,
   thin-sliced scallions,
   thin-sliced radishes

From the day Cami decided she wanted to learn to cook, she chose dishes that seemed completely out of her league. Much to our surprise (because of her young age), she always seemed to pull it off! Pad Thai is one of her favorites. She's the artist in our family, and when she first made it, we realized she loved choosing and creating dishes that had many layers and textures of colors and shapes.

make the sauce

Combine all the sauce ingredients in a medium bowl and whisk well. Set aside.

cook the chicken

Place the chicken in a bowl, season with the garlic powder, onion powder, salt, and pepper, and toss. Heat ¼ cup oil in a large skillet or wok over medium heat. Add the chicken pieces and cook without turning for 3 minutes or until browned. Flip them over and cook until cooked through, about 3 more minutes.

Meanwhile, cook the noodles according to package directions and set aside.

In the same skillet you used for the chicken, heat 3 tablespoons oil over medium heat. Add eggs and cook until scrambled, chopping them into small pieces as they cook. Add the noodles and sauce and stir well. Add the chicken and toss well. Serve with lime wedges for squeezing.

+ added yum: Top each bowl of pad Thai with your choice of toppings.

tip

Serve with sriracha for heat lovers to add to their heart's content.

date-night-in lobster mac + cheese

ready in 1 hour, 10 minutes
serves 2 to 3

This heightened comfort meal makes for a cozy date night in or a small, intimate gathering with friends. You're sure to warm hearts with this special, luxurious, and relaxed meal.

lobster

3 lobster tails (about 5 ounces each, unless you want more!)
2 tablespoons salted butter
1 tablespoon Old Bay seasoning
⅛ teaspoon garlic powder

mac + cheese

8 ounces Banza chickpea penne pasta
3 tablespoons unsalted butter
2 tablespoons all-purpose flour (gluten-free OK)
2 cups half-and-half
¼ teaspoon garlic powder
¼ teaspoon onion powder
2 cups shredded cheddar cheese, divided
1 cup shredded Gruyère cheese, divided
Kosher salt and freshly ground black pepper to taste
⅛ teaspoon nutmeg

panko topping

2 tablespoons unsalted butter
1 cup panko crumbs (gluten-free OK)
¼ cup fresh grated Parmesan cheese

prepare the lobster tails

Preheat the oven to broil. Line a baking sheet with foil.

Using a very sharp knife, cut a line down the center of the softer side of each tail. Place on the foil-lined baking sheet. In a glass bowl, melt the butter in the microwave. Add the Old Bay and garlic powder and stir well. Pour inside the shells, trying to reach all of the lobster meat.

Broil the lobsters for 5 to 8 minutes or until an instant-read thermometer registers 145°F when inserted in the thickest part of the lobster meat. (Timing can vary greatly; it depends on the size of your lobster tails.) When the lobster has cooled, pull the meat from the shells and chop into bite-size pieces. Set aside.

make the mac + cheese

Preheat the oven to 350°F. Spray a 10- or 12-inch baking dish with cooking spray.

Cook the pasta according to package instructions minus 1 minute. Drain and transfer to a large mixing bowl.

Melt the butter in the same pot used to cook the pasta. Whisk in the flour and cook, whisking until lightly browned. Slowly whisk in the half-and-half, then the garlic powder and onion powder. When the mixture is slightly bubbling, add 1 cup of the cheddar and ½ cup of the Gruyère. Whisk well. Add the salt, pepper, and nutmeg and combine well. Add the pasta and stir to coat well.

Pour half of the pasta into the prepared baking dish. Sprinkle the remaining 1 cup cheddar and remaining ½ cup Gruyère on top of

the pasta layer. Top with the rest of the pasta mixture and nestle the lobster pieces into the top layer.

make the topping

In a medium glass bowl, melt the butter in the microwave. Add the panko and Parmesan, coating well with the butter. Sprinkle the crumbs all over the top of the mac + cheese. Bake for 20 minutes or until bubbling.

tips

- This is special enough for an occasion or company.
- Double or triple the recipe!
- The mac + cheese is amazing just as is without lobster!
- You can totally change the personality of this dish into something else very special. Swap out the cheddar cheese for truffle Gouda cheese! OMG too!

down-home backyard shrimp boil

ready in 1 hour, 30 minutes
serves 8

4 teaspoons Old Bay
   seasoning
1 (3-ounce) bag Zatarain's
   crawfish, shrimp,
   and crab boil
2 tablespoons black
   ground pepper
1 tablespoon cayenne pepper
1 tablespoon red
   pepper flakes
3 ounces hot sauce (Franks
   RedHot, Crystal, etc.)
1 (12-ounce) bottle
   beer (any kind)
4 lemons, washed
   and cut in half
6 yellow onions, peeled
   and quartered
3 pounds tiny red and/or
   golden potatoes (4–5 mini
   potatoes/person + extra
   for the pot), washed
12 ears fresh corn,
   cut into thirds
4 to 5 pounds uncooked
   medium shrimp, deveined
   but with shell on
1 cup (2 sticks) unsalted
   butter, melted

The backyard shrimp boil was introduced to us by a neighbor of my sister in Florida, long before Tom and I had kids. I guess you would call theirs a front-yard shrimp boil, because her neighbor set it up on their street and invited all of the neighbors on the block. We look back and are so grateful that we were included because we have incorporated the shrimp boil into the fabric of our lives. We embraced it because it's such a fun and laid-back way to entertain. The shrimp boil process in itself is very entertaining and makes for great party chats around the giant pot.

*For years, we auctioned off shrimp boils at our kids' school to help raise money for computers, books, arts, and sports programs, etc. We would get a few couples to sponsor and throw the party with us. We all donated the ingredients and one of our backyards, and then families who had bought tickets at the auction showed up for the feast. It really put the FUN in **fun**draising! Even though the kids are done with school, we still do shrimp boil parties; now it's just for fun and the tradition that we so enjoyed with friends.*

The beauty of the shrimp boil is the casual, down-home feel. We get the Cajun music rockin' and the cold beverages flowing! We set up family-style dining with long tables and use easy, throw-away food containers.

The few ingredients of shrimp, corn, potatoes, and spices make it a pretty affordable way to throw a party and feed a crowd. We hope you're inspired to try this because you're about to have a lot of fun!

—Sharon

Using at least a 24-quart stockpot with strainer basket (see Tips), fill two-thirds with water. Add the Old Bay, crab boil bag, black pepper, cayenne pepper, red pepper flakes, hot sauce, beer, lemons, and onions and bring to a boil over high heat. Reduce the heat and boil for 15 minutes.

down-home backyard shrimp boil

Add the potatoes and cook for 10 minutes. Add the corn and cook for another 10 minutes. Add the shrimp last, cooking until they turn orange—2 or 3 minutes. Lift the strainer of food out of the water, let drain a bit, and dump into a large tub. (We use a large galvanized tub from Home Depot). Pour the melted butter all over and ring the dinner bell!

tips

- You can easily find a 24-quart classic bayou-type stockpot with a strainer basket online.
- We usually figure about a ½ pound of shrimp per person and then throw some extra in the pot to be safe.
- Pat O'Brien's is an iconic bar in New Orleans known for its signature cocktail, the Hurricane. A quick online search reveals the recipe and some fun history about it. It will definitely get the shrimp boil party started!

Kelsey's housewarming party

tommy p's grilled chicken wings

ready in under 30 minutes
serves 3 to 4

2 tablespoons favorite rub
(we love Meat Church
Honey Hog BBQ rub) or
a mix of salt, pepper,
and garlic powder
30 party chicken wings
½ cup (1 stick) salted butter
½ cup hot sauce of choice
+ **added yum:**
Fries (page 157 or 178),
celery and carrot sticks,
and blue cheese dressing

 **notes**

We have to give credit to the hubby and dad of our family, Tommy P, for these beauties, which have become legendary among friends. In fact, we served them at a backyard birthday for Kelsey a few years ago and her friends still talk about them.

Learning how to make and perfect your favorite pub or brewery food equals the very best nights at home with friends. The wings are a football season go-to in our family. We use a team approach for efficiency and time the prep perfectly at halftime or in between games so we don't miss a thing: TP heads out to the grill with the wings, the girls get sauce, dippers, and fries ready inside. Our wings are not fried or breaded, but after tasting them, you'll never go back to breaded or fried again!

Heat a grill to high. Sprinkle the rub on the wings and let them rest to reach room temperature.

In a large saucepan or soup pot, melt the butter and hot sauce. Set aside.

Grill the wings at 450°F for 15 to 20 minutes (depending on thickness), flipping approximately every 5 minutes or until cooked through. Drop the cooked wings into the sauce mixture. Put the lid on the pot, hold tightly, and give some good shakes to coat all of the wings.

+ **added yum:** Serve with fries, celery and carrot sticks, and blue cheese dressing.

tips

- If you have a smoker, smoke the wings for 1 hour before grilling to add another layer of flavor, and then grill at 350°F for 15 minutes.
- You can use whatever hot sauce you like for this recipe, but we love Frank's RedHot or Crystal.

house-made pizza dough + pizza party inspo

tradition ♥

ready in 2 hours, 20 minutes
serves 5 to 7

1 (¼-ounce) package
    (2¼ teaspoons)
    active dry yeast
¾ cup warm water
1 teaspoon sugar
3 tablespoons extra-virgin
    olive oil
2 cups "00" flour (see Tips)
¾ teaspoon kosher salt

OK, so a pizza party may not be the most relaxing entertaining idea, but it means a fun, lively, interactive evening and the best memories with family and friends! Just keep in mind that you'll be cooking a steady flow of pizzas—so why not make it a family affair and have fun switching up pizza cooking duties? Plus, we've found that guests just love being involved in the process, especially if everyone gets to design and create their own pizza, then share it with the crowd. It's a good way to keep a nice rhythm of feeding people and creates some pretty fun competition! Be sure to serve a salad to satisfy appetites while waiting for more pizza.

Empty the yeast packet in a small bowl and pour the warm water over it. Add the sugar and stir until dissolved. Let sit for 5 minutes. It should start to look foamy.

Brush a large glass bowl with a bit of olive oil. In a standing mixer with dough hook attachment, mix the yeast mixture, remaining oil, flour, and salt until a dough ball is formed. Transfer the dough ball to a floured surface and knead for 1 minute. Place the kneaded dough ball into the greased glass bowl. Cover with plastic wrap and let the dough rise in a warm, dark space until it's doubled in size, about 1 hour. Mark a piece of tape on the outside of the bowl where the dough starts so you can see how much it rises.

Take the dough out and punch air out to form it down into a ball again. At this stage, either store the dough in an airtight container in the refrigerator for later use (up to 24 hours) or cut into dough balls to roll out for pizzas. Divide into five or six balls for personal size pizzas or three balls for small family-size pizzas. On wood cutting boards, roll out each ball into a round that is about ⅓-inch thick, dusting with a little flour to keep the dough from sticking. If you make the rounds too thin, it's hard to transfer the dough and the toppings will make it break apart.

 **notes**

Preheat a conventional oven to 475°F (or follow your pizza oven instructions, usually between 800° and 900°F) with a pizza stone inside if you have one. Have your guests top the pizzas with personal favorites.

Bake the pizzas in a conventional oven for 10 to 15 minutes or in a pizza oven for about 2 minutes. Watch over the pizzas; cooking time will depend on size and amount of toppings.

tips

- Make your dough early in the day so it's ready for pizza party time. Don't roll it too thin, keep it about ⅓-inch in thickness to make transferring it to the oven easier. Don't overload your pizza dough with too much sauce or it will make the dough soggy and break apart. Brush the pizza dough edges with olive oil for nice crisp edges.
- "00" flour is considered the gold standard for pizza crust. It is powder-fine and will make the crust both chewy and crispy in all the right places. It's perfectly OK to use all-purpose flour, but we think it's really worth it to order some 00 flour online ahead of time and keep on hand.
- Parchment paper works well for making and rolling out the dough on your counter and transferring the pizza to the cooking surface.
- Have a couple of pizza stones or multiple rimless baking sheets so you can keep a steady rotation of pizzas being prepared and cooked.
- We have fallen in love with patio pizza parties so much, we eventually got a pizza oven. Not to worry, regular ovens work just great; that's how we did it for many years.

pizza party inspo

Put out all kinds of toppings to make a fun pizza party. You might want to offer up standard pizza fixings of marinara sauce, mozzarella, pepperoni, and sausage. We love to use all kinds of chicken sausages too—check your market for interesting takes, like sundried tomato and Parmesan, spinach and feta, apple, etc.

Also consider less traditional sauces and toppings to wow your friends. You can get creative with pesto and assorted cheeses and meats. We enjoy making a pizza with our spinach-basil pesto (next page) as the base, topping it with sliced peaches, goat cheese, shredded Parm, and fresh basil.

For even less traditional sauces, find quality extra-virgin olive oil, lemon oil, or truffle oil to make "white pizzas." For toppings, look beyond standard mozzarella to burrata, goat cheese, Parmesan cheese, and gorgonzola, along with tomatoes, peppers, broccolini, basil, chives, arugula, spinach, kale, mushrooms, shallots, capers, artichokes, and olives.

herbalicious spinach + basil pesto

ready in 10 minutes
serves 5 to 10

⅓ cup extra-virgin olive oil

2 tablespoons freshly
    squeezed lemon juice

2 to 3 garlic cloves,
    smashed and peeled

1 cup spinach

1 cup fresh basil leaves

¼ cup walnuts

¼ cup grated good
    Parmesan cheese

Kosher salt and freshly
    ground black
    pepper to taste

We love having fresh pesto on hand. It's perfect for homemade pizzas and adds so much fresh, healthy flavor to veggies, pasta, sandwiches, and salads.

In a blender, food processor, or bullet blender, blend the olive oil, lemon juice, garlic, spinach, basil, and walnuts until creamy. Add the Parmesan and pulse until combined well. Season to taste with salt and pepper.

tip

Add water or oil to reach desired texture.

marinated grilled skirt steak + inspo board

ready in 40 minutes
serves 4 to 6

½ cup extra-virgin olive oil

Juice of 1 lemon

½ cup hoisin sauce

¼ cup Worcestershire sauce

¼ cup soy sauce

¼ cup balsamic vinegar

3 garlic cloves, smashed,
    peeled, and chopped

Leaves from 1 sprig fresh
    rosemary leaves, chopped

1½ tablespoons
    garlic powder

1 tablespoon onion powder

1 teaspoon kosher salt

¼ teaspoon black pepper

2 pounds skirt steak

Every juicy steak fan needs a go-to marinade and cut of meat they learn to perfect for their family and friends. Skirt steaks are one of the most flavorful and reliable steaks to build grilling confidence. Like flank steaks, they are thicker in the middle and get thinner toward the ends. We love that because you can please everyone and offer steak slices from medium-rare to well-done—without doing anything extra. This marinade started with a little of this and a little of that and has slowly solidified into our family's go-to—not just for steak, but chicken as well.

In a large resealable bag, combine the olive oil, lemon juice, hoisin, Worcestershire, soy sauce, balsamic, garlic, rosemary, garlic powder, onion powder, salt, and pepper and mix. Add the steak to the bag and remove all the air as you seal it closed. Massage the marinade into the steak. Refrigerate for at least 30 minutes, but no longer than 8 hours.

Preheat the grill to medium heat.

Remove the steak from the marinade and grill for 10 minutes, turning once, or until an instant-read thermometer registers a minimum of 145°F in the thickest part. Let rest for at least 5 minutes before slicing and serving.

grilled steak board inspo

We love steak boards like we love burger boards. The presentation looks lovely and it just says *fun!* When thinking of steak sides you enjoy, also think *simple elegance*. What can easily be prepared ahead of time or while you're grilling? Think of what will present well on the board. Our Grilled Zucchini + Dusted Parm (page 161) or Persimmon Caprese Salad (page 91) are some of our favorites for steak boards. We love watermelon and grilled peach slices too. Baked potatoes are easy and always a big hit. How about grilled asparagus and/or grilled corn? Lettuce wedges with blue cheese dressing are really fun—and easy, too! The possibilities are endless!

party paella

ready in 2 hours
serves 10 to 12

chicken

1 tablespoon sweet or
    smoked paprika
2 teaspoons dried oregano
3 skinless boneless
    chicken breasts
Olive oil for drizzling

paella

⅓ cup Spanish olive oil
1 large Spanish yellow
    onion, chopped
1 red bell pepper, cored,
    seeded, and chopped
6 cloves fresh garlic,
    smashed, peeled,
    and chopped
Leaves from 1 bunch fresh
    flat-leaf parsley, chopped
    (save some for garnish)
1 (15-ounce) can diced
    tomatoes, drained
    and crushed
30 saffron threads
1 (10-ounce) tube package of
    soft Mexican beef chorizo

4 cups short-grain Spanish
    rice (we get the short-
    grain paella rice at Whole
    Foods or Matiz Valenciano
    paella rice from Amazon)
Kosher salt and freshly
    ground black
    pepper to taste
10 cups chicken broth (have
    more on deck, just in case)
2 pounds large shrimp,
    peeled and deveined
2 dozen mussels (clams
    can be used too),
    washed in cold water
2 Spanish chorizo sausages
    (ready to eat), casings
    removed, sliced thick
    on the diagonal
+ added yum:
    Lemon wedges and
    extra parsley for
    beautiful presentation
    and added flavor.

Paella and I began our long romance about 25 years ago when my dear friend, Cristina, invited me to dinner at her house in Florida. When she opened the door to greet me, it smelled like a toasty, warm hug that I remember to this day. I was introduced to paella that night, thanks to her hospitality and Cuban family's delicious cooking.

I love the history of paella's beautiful heritage going back to farmers in Spain. They would make rice lunches out in the fields with whatever food resources were on hand. Its hard-working roots make it a beautifully humble dish, and I admire that.

As for "traditional" paella, I've learned it depends on who you ask. Some say it can have seafood, some say mixed meats only, some say all the above. The many paella "rules," stories, and variety of recipes are part of its charm and I love that too!

My paella love grew to new heights when I visited Kelsey who was studying in Spain. It seemed that every restaurant had it on the menu, and each time I dared myself to try something new, a

Annual summer paella party in our backyard

party paella

waiter would walk by with a paella that looked quite different from the one I had in the town before. So I had to order it. The reason it never got old, I quickly learned, is that paella is not only a pan of fresh ingredients exclusive to its town, it was an artistic canvas for the crafter. I really relate to that: Each paella reflects the heart, resources, and creativity of the chef.

I have been making paella now for many years. I've tweaked and enhanced my recipe every time I've had it in a different place from a different person. When the girls were little, they didn't care much for seafood, so it became a romantic dinner for two on Valentine's Day or a date night for Tom and me. Although it's cozy and perfect for a couple, paella is truly a dish of love and deserves to be shared with many! It's a perfect centerpiece for gatherings and celebrations.

After years of making paella in my cast iron skillet or Dutch oven, I decided it was time for a real paella pan. I was on the chase for being able to create the socarrat, the toasted, crusty, rice-bottom technique that can really only be achieved in an authentic paella pan because of its unique shape. So I went online to get myself a real paella pan. I found a really fun website (tienda.com), and in my excitement, I placed my order without paying enough attention.

Fast forward—a giiiiigantic box arrived on our doorstep. My hubby was the first to find it. Intrigued by what I could have ordered that was so big, he stood by as I sheepishly opened the box. We both laughed hysterically as I pulled out my new, gigantic, 36-inch paella pan! Oops! Of course, I intended to be able to make paella for company, but the size of this pan took Paella Party to a whole new level. Oh well, what's wrong with that, anyway?

So, if you're going to have a party-level paella pan, you have to have a paella party, right? That's exactly what we've done ever since the big pan arrived. Each year, we invite some of our dearest friends to come help us make and eat it. It's so fun to have friends gathered around the pan talking, helping, and laughing as it all comes together. It has become one of our favorite friends and family traditions. What I especially love is that Kelsey, Kendall, and Cami's friends love the tradition just as much as we do. They always ask for this year's date,

and that just warms our hearts; while I might have thought I didn't order the right paella pan, the right paella pan found us!

If you've never made paella, I hope this inspires you to give it a try with whatever pan you have. You can start small with the recipe we've given. If you love the taste and process, maybe you'll get a larger pan size, scale up the recipe, and start a paella party tradition of your own. (Just keep in mind, the bigger the pan, the more burners needed. And be sure to have extra broth on deck: Paella seems to require more liquid when making larger batches.) There is something very special about paella. I can't explain it, but you'll feel it and be so glad you know how to make it.

—Sharon

cook the chicken

Heat the oven to 350°F. Mix the paprika and oregano and rub all over the chicken. Cover and marinate for at least an hour in the refrigerator. Place in a small baking dish and drizzle with a little oil. Bake for 25 minutes (depending on the size and thickness) or until cooked through or an instant-read thermometer registers 165°F when inserted in a thick part of one breast. Let cool, then cut into bite-size pieces. You can do this 1 or 2 days ahead.

make the paella

Heat the oil in a 20-inch paella pan over medium heat. Start by making the *sofrito:* Add the onion, pepper, garlic, and parsley and cook for 2 to 3 minutes. Add the tomatoes and saffron and blend well until everything starts caramelizing a bit, about 5 minutes.

Add the tubed chorizo and stir well. Add the rice, coating it well as you stir. Pour in the broth and bring to a simmer. Reduce the heat and simmer, moving the pan often to help cook evenly and prevent burning until almost all of the liquid is absorbed. Test rice for *almost* doneness and add another cup of broth if needed. The rice should be approaching tender and almost done before adding the uncooked seafood. The rice will continue cooking with seafood, but it should be almost done before adding. Add the shrimp and mussels, tucking them cozy into the rice to help them cook. Cook until the shrimp are bright orange and cooked through. This should take 5 to 7 minutes, and the mussels should open during that time. (Discard any mussels that don't open.)

Add the cooked chicken and sliced chorizo and cook until warmed through. Let everything simmer together in the pan, without stirring, for 5 minutes.

When the seafood is cooked and the rice is tender, turn up the heat for 30 to 45 seconds or until you can smell the rice toasting at the bottom. That's the *socarrat,* the crispy bottom layer that is the signature of the paella! Remove from heat and rest for 5 minutes. Sprinkle with additional parsley and squeeze the lemon wedges on top right before serving.

The paella process will probably take an hour from start to finish.

red wine-braised short ribs

**ready in 3 hours, 30 minutes
serves 4 to 6**

½ cup all-purpose
    flour of choice
1 tablespoon garlic powder
Kosher salt and freshly
    ground black pepper
4 to 5 pounds bone-
    in beef short ribs (or
    about 2 ribs per person,
    depending on size)
2 tablespoons extra-virgin
    olive oil, plus more
    if needed
1 (5-ounce) package uncured
    chopped pancetta
1 large sweet yellow
    onion, chopped
4 whole carrots, peeled and
    chopped into 1-inch pieces
2 shallots, sliced thin
4 cloves garlic, smashed,
    peeled, and chopped
Leaves from 3 sprigs fresh
    rosemary, chopped
Leaves from 3 sprigs
    fresh thyme
2½ cups red wine (preferably
    Cabernet Sauvignon)
2 tablespoons tomato paste
3 cups beef broth

As we've said, we love serving comfort food to our friends! Wine-braised short ribs have elegant flavors similar to beef bourguignon and make the perfect elevated dinner party food. We always say no one likes an uptight hostess—this recipe is the antidote; it's assembled and cooked before your guests even arrive, allowing you to be relaxed and ready for fun. And the slow cook in the oven makes it practically foolproof. Serve on top of our Creamy, Dreamy, Cheesy Polenta (page 149) or Russet + Sweet Potato Mashup (page 162), and drizzle a couple of spoonsful of the juicy sauce on top. You'll have your guests asking where you received chef training.

Preheat the oven to 350°F.

In a resealable plastic bag, combine the flour, garlic powder, and salt and pepper to taste. Shake well to mix. Add the short ribs, seal, and shake to coat well.

Heat the olive oil in a large Dutch oven over medium heat. Add the pancetta and cook until crispy, 4 to 5 minutes. Remove the pancetta with a slotted spoon and set aside in a large bowl.

In the same pot over medium-high heat, brown the short ribs, about 1 minute on all sides. Transfer the browned short ribs to the bowl with pancetta. To the same Dutch oven, add the onion, carrots, and shallots; add a little more oil if needed. Sauté over medium-high heat until the onion starts to lightly brown. Add the garlic, rosemary, and thyme and cook until you smell the garlic, 1 to 2 minutes. Remove from the pot from the heat.

Carefully add the wine, tomato paste, and broth. Return to heat and stir well, getting all of the crispy bits up from the bottom. Add the short ribs and pancetta. Bring to a boil, cover, and transfer to the oven. Bake for 2 hours. Reduce the heat to 325°F and bake for another 30 minutes or until the ribs are tender and ready to fall off the bone. Let it rest for 20 to 30 minutes. Skim any fat off the top with a large spoon before serving.

tip

Don't overcoat the meat with flour; you don't want the flour to burn while browning. Turn down heat immediately if it starts getting too brown.

sexy slow cooker asian-inspired friday-night lettuce wraps

complete meal

**Prep is 30 minutes
ready in 2 hours on high
(4½ hours on low)
serves 4 to 6**

2 pounds ground chicken
1¼ cups hoisin sauce
½ cup reduced-sodium tamari
2 tablespoons rice vinegar
1½ tablespoons sesame oil
1 tablespoon extra-virgin
    olive oil
1½ tablespoons sriracha
1 tablespoon brown sugar
1 tablespoon grated
    fresh ginger
4 cloves garlic, smashed,
    peeled, and chopped
1¼ teaspoons 5-spice blend
¼ cup cornstarch
1 cup finely chopped
    cremini mushrooms
1½ cups grated carrots
1 bunch scallions (white and
    green parts), sliced thin
2 heads butter lettuce
2 (8-ounce) cans water
    chestnuts, drained
    and chopped
+ added yum for serving:
    Fresh cilantro, sliced
    scallion tops, grated raw
    carrot, and sweet chili
    sauce, optional for dipping

Who doesn't love making and eating lettuce wraps? This recipe is perfect after a busy week but still want to have friends over for some Friday night fun. It's easy, delicious, and very festive! Everything can be prepped the night or morning before; then it all comes together quickly.

If you set out some sides like edamame, cashews, and mandarin oranges, there's no need to provide a fancy appetizer too. When your guests arrive, they can serve themselves and you can sit back and enjoy a relaxed evening with your friends.

Place the ground chicken in a medium bowl, cover with plastic wrap, and microwave for 8 minutes. Stir and break up the meat just a little after about 4 minutes. (Leave the meat a little on the chunky side so that it doesn't become mushy in the slow cooker. You can break it up more right before serving.)

Turn the slow cooker on high. Add the hoisin, tamari, vinegar, sesame oil, olive oil, sriracha, brown sugar, ginger, garlic, and 5-spice and mix until well combined. Whisk in the cornstarch. Stir in the mushrooms, carrots, and scallions, then add the cooked chicken. Cover and cook on high for 2 hours (or low for 4 to 5 hours).

While the chicken mixture is cooking, carefully remove the leaves from the butter lettuce head one at a time so you do not rip them. Wash well and put them in a colander, leaving them wet. Store in the refrigerator until dinner time. Dry the lettuce leaves before serving.

Roughly chop the water chestnuts, leaving them in big enough chunks to add texture and a nice crunch. Stir them into the crockpot chicken mixture right before serving. Garnish the chicken with cilantro and additional scallions.

Set the slow cooker bowl on the counter along with the lettuce leaves and **+ added yum** for guests to make their own lettuce wraps.

sexy slow cooker mojo pulled pork

Prep is 15 minutes
ready in 8 hours on low
(5 to 6 hours on high)
serves 6 to 8

3 to 4 pounds boneless
    pork shoulder
¾ cup sour orange juice
½ cup extra-virgin olive oil
¼ cup lime juice
2 yellow onions, halved
    and sliced thin
12 cloves fresh garlic,
    smashed, peeled,
    and chopped
2½ teaspoons ground cumin
2 teaspoons dried oregano
1 teaspoon kosher salt
Freshly ground black pepper

 **notes**

Cuban pulled pork is another family favorite. Slow roasting in the oven is hard to beat, but when you love it as much as our family, you figure out how to make it with a little less attention so you can have it more often.

Mojo is a Cuban-style marinade—the key to the pulled pork's success! It's easy to whip up, but finding the necessary sour orange juice isn't easy in all parts of the country. It's available at Latin supermarkets or online. (We love the Goya brand.) Using boneless pork shoulder creates the succulence you'll dream about. Serve with Quick + Easy Cuban-Style Black Beans (page 182), Russet + Sweet Potato Mashup (page 162), Cumin + Cotija Street Fries (page 158), or white rice of choice. Also delicious in tacos or on top of nachos!

Turn the slow cooker on low.

Cut slits into the pork shoulder all over with a sharp paring knife. Whisk together all the remaining ingredients in the slow cooker. Add the pork and coat well. Cover and cook 8 hours on low or 5 to 6 hours on high. If you're home, flip the meat after 3 or 4 hours. (It will still be delicious if you can't.)

Use two forks to pull the meat apart before serving.

tofu spring rolls

plant forward

complete meal

ready in 45 minutes
serves 4 (can be scaled
up or down)

peanut sauce

5 tablespoons smooth
peanut butter
4 teaspoons lime juice
2 teaspoons soy
sauce or tamari
1 teaspoon sesame oil
2 cloves fresh garlic,
smashed, peeled, and
chopped finely
½ teaspoon ground ginger
Water for desired consistency
Sriracha to taste

spring rolls

8 ounces firm tofu, drained
and sliced into strips
2 leaves purple
cabbage, sliced
2 medium carrots, julienned
½ cup snap peas, chopped
1 avocado, pitted,
peeled, and sliced
8 fresh mint leaves, chopped
½ cup finely chopped
fresh cilantro
2 ounces rice noodles
8 sheets rice paper

If you're trying to get creative and include more plant protein in your life, tofu is something to try. Basically compressed soybeans, tofu is a complete protein, meaning it contains all of the essential amino acids we need. It is also a good plant-based source of iron.

Not everyone in our family embraced tofu at the same time, but we all love making creative and delicious spring rolls. So our trusty dietitian Kendall encouraged us to slip tofu into the party mix! The so-called tofu haters actually loved it in these salad rolls. The flavors fit perfectly with the crunchiness of the fresh veggies. The dipping sauce puts it over the top. This is something fun to do with friends for a happy hour. Like tacos, is it more fun making them or eating them? We say both!

make the peanut sauce

In a medium bowl, combine the peanut butter, lime juice, soy sauce, sesame oil, garlic, and ground ginger and whisk to combine well. Add water in teaspoon increments until desired consistency. Add sriracha to desired spice level.

make the rolls

Wrap the tofu in a dish towel or paper towel and place something heavy on top to drain excess water for 10 to 15 minutes.

While the tofu is draining, arrange the cabbage, carrots, snap peas, avocado, mint, and cilantro on a pretty board or plate. Set aside.

Cook the rice noodles according to package instructions. Drain (no need to rinse) and add noodles to the board. Slice the drained tofu into strips and add to the board.

Fill a large bowl with room-temperature water. Carefully place one sheet of rice paper in the bowl and soak for 10 to 15 seconds. (Various rice paper brands may have different instructions; see package for best results.) Remove the rice paper from the water and lay flat on a large plate. Add one-eighth of each prepared filling. Roll up as tightly as possible. Repeat with each piece of rice paper to make eight rolls.

Serve the spring rolls with the peanut sauce.

tip

If you have peanut allergies in your house as we do, substitute another butter like cashew or sunflower seed butter in the peanut sauce. We have done both and it makes a delicious dipping sauce!

 **notes**

sweets + treats

We believe that food has no moral value, therefore, there are no "good" or "bad" foods, nor is a person "good" or "bad" for eating certain foods. Some foods nourish our minds and bodies, others have ways to nourish our souls. Food should be a source of joy rather than a source of guilt, shame, or stress. Too often, sweets are often labeled as "indulgent," "bad," or "naughty," but we believe that sweets and treats should always have a place in our lives, and we should feel free to enjoy these foods as we see fit. The smell and taste of a fresh-baked chocolate chip cookie are sometimes just what our soul needs.

aunt dale's blueberry hubby delight

tradition

ready in 2 hours
serves 10 to 12

crust

¾ cup self-rising flour

¼ cup all-purpose flour

1 cup pecans, chopped
   very fine

½ cup (1 stick) unsalted
   butter, melted

blueberry filling

3 cups fresh blueberries,
   washed and drained

¾ cup granulated sugar

¼ cup water

1 teaspoon lemon juice

1 tablespoon cornstarch

1 (8-ounce) package cream
   cheese, softened

1 cup powdered sugar

1 (8-ounce) container
   Cool Whip

Our adorable Aunt Dale is 91 years strong and known for her special icebox cake. It's become her calling card when she brings the refreshing blueberry delight to the homebound in her community and to church gatherings. She jokes that her senior citizens' club won't let her in the door for their potlucks without it. She has many blueberry bushes on her property in Alabama, which is what prompted her to begin making this for her beloved hubby, Bartis, years ago. (Shhhh, don't tell anyone, but Aunt Dale doesn't even like blueberries.)

Important note: *Both the crust and filling need to be made well in advance of assembling and serving to allow both to cool completely.*

make the crust

Preheat the oven to 350°F.

In a medium bowl, combine the self-rising flour, all-purpose flour, and pecans. Add the melted butter and mix to make a dough. This can be done by hand, in a food processor, or in a stand mixer with the paddle attachment. Press the dough onto the bottom of a 9 x 13-inch baking pan. Bake until the crust is light brown, about 20 minutes. Allow to cool completely.

make the filling

Cook the blueberries, granulated sugar, and water in a medium saucepan over medium heat, stirring occasionally or until about half the blueberries start to break down, 6 to 8 minutes. Whisk in the lemon juice and cornstarch, combining well, then stir until the liquid thickens, 2 to 3 minutes. Remove from heat and allow to cool completely.

assemble the delight

Mix together the cream cheese and powdered sugar in a medium bowl. (An electric hand mixer also works well.) Spread over the cooled crust. Pour the blueberry filling on top of the cream cheese mixture and finish with Cool Whip. Place in the fridge to solidify, 2 to 3 hours (or 30 to 45 minutes in the freezer). Store in the freezer for up to two weeks; thaw on the counter for a few minutes before serving.

tip

A 21-ounce can of blueberry pie filling can be substituted for the blueberry filling, or substitute any flavor pudding for the filling; you have endless possibilities. We especially love chocolate or banana pudding when fresh blueberries aren't readily available.

♡ notes

berry delicious crisp

ready in 40 minutes
serves 8 to 10

5 tablespoons
   unsalted butter
1½ cups favorite granola
1½ cups quick-cooking
   rolled oats (we use
   Bob's Red Mill)
1 cup packed brown sugar
4 cups mixed berries
3 tablespoons apple
   juice (OJ works too)
Juice of ½ lemon
+ added yum:
   Vanilla ice cream

 **notes**

It's a blast to go berry picking in Oregon, and over the years, we've had fun figuring out creative ways to use berries—from desserts and jams to salads and margaritas. This berry crisp is one of our all-time favorites. Wait until you smell it baking and feel the coziness it brings to your heart and home. The basic recipe works with every kind of berry, plus peach, apple, and pears too, so you can change its personality with the seasons!

Preheat the oven to 375°F. Lightly spray a large baking or casserole dish with cooking spray.

In a large bowl, microwave the butter until melted. Add the granola, oats, and brown sugar and mix to combine.

Combine the berries, apple juice, and lemon juice in the prepared baking dish. Top with granola mixture. Bake for 25 to 30 minutes or until the top is a nice golden brown. This will keep in the refrigerator for three to four days.

+ **added yum:** Serve with a generous scoop of vanilla bean ice cream!

tip

This is also delicious on your morning yogurt.

blood orange + yogurt + olive oil pound cake

This cake is so beautiful and perfect for Easter, a baby shower, a tea party, or just to nurture yourself! Citrus-fresh and incredibly moist, it looks and feels like all the joys of spring.

cake

All-purpose flour and
    vegetable oil for the pan
1½ cups all-purpose flour
2 teaspoons baking powder
½ teaspoon kosher salt
Grated zest and ⅓ cup juice
    from 2 blood oranges
1 cup granulated sugar
3 large eggs
1 cup Greek vanilla yogurt
1½ teaspoons vanilla extract
½ cup extra-virgin olive oil

candied orange slices

1 blood orange
½ cup granulated sugar
½ water

pink glaze

1½ cups powdered sugar
3 to 4 tablespoons fresh-
    squeezed blood
    orange juice

make the cake

Preheat the oven to 350°F. Lightly oil a standard Bundt pan and dust lightly with flour.

Blend the flour, baking powder, and salt in a medium glass bowl. Combine the zest and juice, granulated sugar, eggs, yogurt, and vanilla in a bowl of a stand mixer. Whisk until well combined and foamy. Add the flour mixture slowly, whisking until blended well. Add the olive oil until smoothly combined.

Pour the batter into the prepared Bundt pan. Bake for 50 to 55 minutes or until a toothpick inserted in the center comes out clean. Let the cake cool.

make the candied orange slices

Wash and dry the orange well. Cut the orange into thin slices and remove all the seeds. Heat the granulated sugar and water in a medium pan over medium-high heat, stirring slowly. When the sugar is dissolved, turn the heat to low and add the orange slices. Simmer for 15 to 20 minutes or until both sides of each slice are candied. If necessary, move them around to keep them separated. They should look almost transparent and the liquid will be dark pink/red and thick. Remove the orange slices from the sugar mix, allowing the excess to drip off the oranges. Place on parchment paper to cool.

make the glaze

While the cake and orange slices are cooling, place the powdered sugar in a medium bowl. While whisking, slowly add the juice until desired glazing texture. It should be able to glide easily over cake but not be too runny.

Place the cake on a cake stand or platter. Drizzle the glaze over the cake, allowing it to drip down over the sides. Arrange the candied oranges on the top. The glaze should set fairly quickly. Once set, it's ready to serve!

notes

browned butter toffee cookies

tradition

ready in 45 minutes
makes about 2 dozen

toffee

1 cup (2 sticks)
   unsalted butter
1 cup granulated sugar
½ teaspoon salt
1 teaspoon vanilla extract
1 cup chocolate chips

cookies

1 cup (2 sticks)
   unsalted butter
2 cups all-purpose flour
1 teaspoon baking soda
½ teaspoon salt
1 cup packed brown sugar
⅓ cup granulated sugar
2 large eggs
2 teaspoons vanilla extract
Chopped toffee (see Tip)
1 cup chocolate chips
Flaky sea salt to top

We've hosted an annual mother & daughter cookie exchange with dear friends for 22 years. It's been one of our favorite traditions; it was so special to watch all of the girls grow up together. We've never made it a contest, however. The only challenge is that all of the mother/daughter teams keep creating beautiful and special cookies that everyone loves. We think this cookie deserves to be out in the universe and at cookie exchanges everywhere.

make the toffee

Line a 9 x 13-inch baking dish with parchment paper.

Place the butter, granulated sugar, and salt in a medium pan and heat over medium heat, stirring continuously to dissolve sugar. Once the mixture reaches a boil, place a candy thermometer in the pot, making sure that it does not touch the bottom. Cook, stirring occasionally, or until the thermometer registers 300°F. Remove the pan from the heat, add the vanilla, and stir. Pour the toffee mixture into the lined baking dish and let sit and cool to room temperature.

Melt the chocolate chips in the microwave for about 1 minute (add 30 seconds at time if necessary) and drizzle it over the toffee, then smooth it out gently with a spatula. Place in the fridge to cool completely, about 15 minutes. Chop the toffee to desired size with a sharp knife. You can store the toffee in a sealed container on the counter for one week, or in the refrigerator for up to two weeks.

make the cookies

Preheat the oven to 375°F. Line two cookie sheets with parchment paper.

Cook the butter in a saucepan over medium heat, stirring often or until it foams and turns brown, 5 to 8 minutes. Remove from heat.

Combine the flour, baking soda, and salt in a medium bowl. Combine the browned butter, brown sugar, and granulated sugar in a large bowl and mix well. Add the eggs and vanilla and mix again until combined. Add the dry ingredients gradually, mixing as you go. Once the wet and dry ingredients are thoroughly incorporated, stir in the toffee pieces and chocolate chips.

Drop portions of dough (balls of about 2½ tablespoons each) onto the prepared cookie sheets, placing them 3 inches apart. Bake the cookies for 9 to 10 minutes or until the edges are golden brown and the centers are soft and gooey. Sprinkle the cookies with flaky sea salt.

tip

There's no "right" amount of toffee here; use as much or as little as you want! We probably use about half of the toffee and save the rest for an extra treat.

♡ notes

darrell + sharon's triple-chip, double-nut cookies

tradition

ready in 30 minutes
makes 3 to 4 dozen

1 cup shortening (or
  butter, if preferred)
½ cup granulated sugar
1 cup packed dark
  brown sugar
1½ teaspoons vanilla extract
2 large eggs, room
  temperature
2¼ cups all-purpose flour
1 teaspoon salt
1 teaspoon baking soda
1 (12-ounce) package
  semisweet or dark
  chocolate chips
1 cup (6-ounce package)
  butterscotch chips
1 cup (6-ounce package)
  white chocolate chips
¾ cup chopped pecans
¾ cup chopped walnuts

 **notes**

My dad was a great baker and fisherman. My favorite memories of him are either in the kitchen or on the water. If the fish weren't biting, he'd take out his thermos of coffee and offer up cookies because he believed it would change the energy of fish. When his coffee break was over, the big ones would be biting for sure.

His chocolate chip cookies always tasted better than anyone else's. When I asked why, he'd say, "It's just the recipe on the back of the chips package, plus a little extra of the good stuff." So I have kept adding a little more of the "good stuff" over the years. I feel close to him every time I make these. I love how a recipe can do that for us.

—Sharon

Preheat the oven to 375°F. Line two cookie sheets with parchment paper.

In a standing mixer with the paddle attachment, cream the shortening, granulated sugar, brown sugar, and vanilla. Add the eggs and beat well.

In a medium bowl, mix the flour, salt, and baking soda well. Still beating the shortening mixture, gradually add the dry ingredients until incorporated. Add all the chips and nuts and blend on low until combined.

Using a medium cookie scoop, drop portions of dough (balls of about 1½ tablespoons each) onto the prepared cookie sheets, placing them at least 3 inches apart. Bake for 9 to 11 minutes or until golden brown. For best results, bake one batch at a time. You can bake two sheets at a time if you switch racks halfway through.

tip

These cookies are also delicious gluten-free. We substitute Cup4Cup gluten-free flour or Bob's Red Mill Gluten-Free 1-to-1 Baking Flour for the all-purpose.

easy peasy gluten-free pie crust

ready in 4 hours, 10 minutes
makes 1 (9-inch) pie crust

1¼ cups multi-purpose
    gluten-free flour (we
    love Cup4cup)
½ teaspoon sugar
½ teaspoon kosher salt
½ cup (1 stick) unsalted
    butter, cut into
    1-tablespoon pieces
¼ cup cold water

Most everyone who's had this pie crust for the first time had no idea it was gluten-free and often complimented the crust as much as the pie itself. Shhhh ;)

One thing I have learned about being allergic to wheat is that eating gluten-free isn't really that big of a deal. I've been happy to realize that the plain ole white flour that was a staple of my existence isn't the only answer for cooking and baking. Gluten-free flours (they are all very different) can sometimes feel like better options for certain recipes because they can create superior texture. This pie crust is a great example.

Making perfect pie crusts can be intimidating. I never had consistent success until I started using a food processor. If you have one, this will be one of the easiest, most reliable pie crust recipes you will ever have.

—Sharon

Add the flour, sugar, and salt to a food processor. Pulse a few times to combine the ingredients. Add the butter piece by piece, pulsing on and off until the mixture looks scraggly and grainy. Slowly add the water until it looks like uniform dough. Don't over pulse. Check to see if you can form a dough ball in your fingers. Use a small amount of additional water if needed to make the dough form.

Lay a piece of plastic wrap on your counter and place the dough on top. Wrap the dough and form into a ball, then press it down to make a fat disc. Refrigerate 4 hours or up to one week.

If the dough is a little too firm when ready to roll, let it sit for a few minutes. With a rolling pin, roll out the dough with patience, rotating the pin to keep the dough a uniform thickness and not crack the edges. When you have about an 11-inch round (a bit bigger than your pie pan), transfer it to the pan and place in the center. Lightly maneuver the dough around to fit the pie pan evenly and allow the dough to drape over the pan (about an inch) for crimping or for joining a top crust (if you've doubled the recipe for a top crust).

Add your filling and bake according to your pie recipe. Cover the pie to include the crust's edges with a sheet of foil once it starts to become golden brown to avoid burning.

tip

For pie recipes that have fillings that are not cooked at all, the pie shell can be pre-baked (a.k.a. *blind baked*): Line the shell with foil and weight it with a few cups of sugar spread evenly or another glass pie plate to prevent the crust sides from shrinking or losing shape and the center from bubbling up. Bake 25 minutes, then remove the foil and weights and bake for another 10 minutes. Let cool, pour the filling into your baked shell, and refrigerate until set.

 **notes**

pecan + bourbon + chocolate chip pie

tradition
♡

ready in 1 hour, 15 minutes

serves 6 to 8

½ cup granulated sugar

½ cup packed brown sugar

1 cup dark corn syrup

¼ cup bourbon (optional)

6 tablespoons unsalted
butter, melted and cooled

3 large eggs

1 teaspoon vanilla extract

½ teaspoon kosher salt

1½ cups whole pecans

⅔ cup semisweet
chocolate chips

1 (9-inch) unbaked pie
shell of choice, or Easy
Peasy (Gluten-Free)
Pie Crust (page 288)

+ added yum:
Whipped cream or
vanilla ice cream

◊ **notes**

Pecan pie is a Thanksgiving classic, but this one deserves more than a once-a-year appearance. Ooey, gooey, rich, and crunchy with subtle bourbon undertones, few pies taste as sophisticated as this one. The pronunciation of pecan always makes for fun table conversation too. Do you say PEE-con, PAH-con, pe-CON, or PEE-can? Did we miss any?

Preheat the oven to 350°F.

In a medium saucepan, combine the granulated sugar, brown sugar, corn syrup, and bourbon. Bring to a boil over medium-high heat and cook until thickened, about 3 minutes. Remove from heat.

In a medium bowl, whisk the cooled, melted butter with the eggs, vanilla, and salt. Then whisk this mixture into the sugar mixture and add the pecans.

Scatter the chocolate chips all around the bottom of the pie shell. Pour in the filling. Using a fork, pull the pecans up to the surface, then flip them over so they all have their backs/lines facing up. It's so pretty, it's totally worth it! We kick out any pecans that aren't completely whole.

Cover the pie with foil and bake on the center rack for 30 minutes. Remove the foil and bake for another 30 minutes or until the center of the pie filling reaches 200°F on an instant-read thermometer and is set. Let cool 2 hours before serving.

+ added yum: Top with whipped cream or vanilla ice cream.

tip

Bake the pie on a foil-covered baking sheet. The pie always drips on the way to the oven or boils over a bit while baking. You'll thank us at cleanup time.

flourless chocolate torte

**ready in 1 hour,
    15 minutes (plus time
    to set and cool)**
serves 16 to 20

torte

1 cup water
¾ cup sugar
9 tablespoons salted
    butter, cut up, plus
    more for the pan
18 ounces, bittersweet
    chocolate, chopped
    (about 2½ cups)
6 large eggs

ganache

1 cup heavy whipping cream
1¼ cup semisweet
    chocolate chips
+ added yum:
    Fresh whipped cream

To say this torte is decadent is an understatement. If you are a chocolate lover, you just might say you've never had a better chocolate anything, anywhere! It is bakery-worthy: Whenever we serve it, friends ask where they can buy it. The best part? It's naturally gluten-free. But note that it is very rich, so modest slivers are key.

make the cake

Preheat the oven to 350°F. Prepare a 10-inch springform pan by greasing the bottom and sides with butter, then lining the bottom with a round of parchment paper. Wrap the outside of the pan with 3 layers of heavy-duty foil, bringing the foil to the top of the rim.

In a small saucepan, bring the water and sugar to boil over medium heat. Stir well until the sugar dissolves, then simmer for 5 minutes. Remove from heat.

In a large saucepan, melt the butter over low heat. Add the chocolate and whisk until smooth. Whisk the sugar syrup into the chocolate. Let it cool slightly. Add the eggs and whisk until well blended.

Pour the batter into the prepared springform pan. Place the pan in a large roasting pan and carefully fill the roasting pan with enough hot water to come halfway up the sides of the springform pan.

Bake the cake for 50 minutes or until the center no longer jiggles when you give it a gentle shake. Carefully remove the cake from its water bath and let it cool completely in the springform pan.

make the ganache

Place the cream and chocolate in a large glass bowl and heat in the microwave, about 30 seconds at a time, or until the chocolate starts melting. Whisk it well until melted, creamy, and smooth.

Pour the ganache mixture evenly all over the top of the cooled cake. Let the cake set in the refrigerator for at least 2 hours, or up to 2 days.

+ added yum: Serve with a good dollop of fresh whipped cream.

tip

This torte is so rich and decadent, a sliver is wonderfully satisfying and allows you to make one dessert for a lot of people!

 notes

grilled banana splits

tradition ♥

ready in 20 minutes
serves 1 (easy to scale up)

1 unpeeled banana

2 tablespoons semisweet
    chocolate chips

2 tablespoons
    butterscotch chips

Ice cream of choice
    (we love a salted caramel
    or butter pecan)

+ added yum:
    Chocolate fudge topping

 **notes**

Think Bananas Foster, with a twist. In the heat of the fire, the bananas break down, caramelize, and mix with chocolate and butterscotch chips, giving us oh-so-fancy vibes. Then we serve them over ice cream for extra decadence—and even add hot fudge! You can cook the wrapped bananas over an open flame with a marshmallow skewer or simply put them on a hot grill. Easy breezy, banana squeezy!

The beauty of the dessert and recipe is its simplicity. That's why we are giving you a one-serving version, as it is super easy to multiply it up for any number of people.

Prepare a grill for medium heat. Cut one 12-inch square of aluminum foil.

Using a sharp knife, make a slit down the length of the banana (on the inside curve), cutting *almost* to the peel on the other side to create a long well. Combine the chocolate and butterscotch chips, tuck them into the banana's slit, then wrap the banana in foil. Grill for 10 to 12 minutes without turning or until the banana is softened and the chips are melted. Carefully open to check about halfway through so you can see how hot and fast they are cooking on your grill.

To serve, scoop ice cream into bowls. Slide the soft banana halves out of the peel and foil (be careful of steam!) and into a bowl.

+ added yum: Drizzle with chocolate fudge.

tips

• Perfect for company! The bananas can be prepped and wrapped hours before your meal. Or get family and friends involved in the cooking process and have each guest assemble their own banana split.

- To keep the bananas upright on the grill (so the filling doesn't ooze out), place one banana leaning against the side of the grill and then place the others side by side to steady each other. And if you have a wide-spaced grate, you can nestle them in between the grating for sturdiness.
- You can also bake the wrapped bananas in a 350°F oven for 10 to 15 minutes.

mimie's amalgamation cake

tradition ♥

ready in 1 hour, 30 minutes
serves 10 to 12

cake

1 cup (2 sticks)
   unsalted butter

2 cups sugar

1 cup sweet milk
   ("whole milk" today)

1 teaspoon vanilla

3 cups all-purpose flour

2 level tablespoons
   baking powder

2 pinches baking soda

2 pinches salt

8 large egg whites (save
   yolks for filling)

filling

8 large egg yolks

2 cups sugar

1 cup (2 sticks)
   unsalted butter

1 cup grated fresh
   coconut (see Tip)

1 cup raisins

2 cups pecans

This decadent, three-layer cake has a long history in the Mississippi Caldwell side of the family as Mimie (Sharon's grandmother) made it for every holiday and special occasion. We'll bet it's like nothing you've ever tasted. When you look at the list of ingredients you can't help but wonder how they will all come together. "Amalgamation" literally means the process of uniting things together and, oh my, it sure does. This vintage cake is unique and will always be in style.

Mimie taught us that we didn't need money to have class and good manners. This regal cake is a true legacy of her elegance and loving lessons.

make the cake

Preheat the oven 350°F. Line the bottom of three 9 x 2-inch round cake pans with parchment paper rounds.

Using an electric mixer, cream the butter well in a large mixing bowl. Gradually add the sugar, still beating until it's a pale yellow. Add the milk, vanilla, and mix well.

In a medium bowl, sift together the flour, baking powder, baking soda, and salt. Slowly add the dry ingredients to the butter mixture and mix to thoroughly combine.

Using the electric mixer with clean beaters in a second bowl, beat the egg whites until stiff peaks form. Be patient, it will take 3 to 5 minutes. Whisk 1 cup of the beaten egg whites into the butter mixture in the large bowl. Then softly keep folding in the rest of the egg whites until the foam is just incorporated. Don't overdo it.

Divide the batter among the three prepared pans. Bake for 30 minutes or until the tops are slightly golden and a toothpick inserted into the center of cake comes out clean. Cool completely.

make the filling

In the top of a double boiler over medium heat, whisk the egg yolks, sugar, and butter. Cook, stirring constantly for 12 to 15 minutes until it's thick and gooey. Increase the heat if needed to get a gooey, sticky consistency. Remove from heat and add the coconut, raisins, and pecans. Let the filling sit for a couple of minutes to ensure consistency that will not run off the cake.

assemble the cake

Place one cake layer on a cake stand or platter and spread about one-third of the filling on top, letting it drip over the sides. Top with a second layer and more filling, letting it drip over that layer, then place the final layer. Spread the remaining filling on the top and let it drip over the sides and spread around. Store in the refrigerator for up to three days.

tip

We shred fresh coconut for this cake because that is what our Grandma Mimie and Aunt Dale did. Packaged, shredded coconut works well and is a great shortcut, but if it's a special occasion, we always use fresh. It's worth the extra effort because it tastes so fresh and creamy and really puts this cake over the top!

 **notes**

quick + easy no-bake oatmeal bars

ready in 30 minutes
(plus time to set)
serves 10

1 cup (2 sticks)
 unsalted butter
⅔ cup packed dark
 brown sugar
1½ teaspoons vanilla extract
3½ cups quick-cooking rolled
 oats (we use gluten-free)
1 cup dark chocolate chips
½ cup sunflower seed butter

♡ **notes**

There is something so satisfying about cookie bars. They hold up well on the go and are a perfect, tasty energy snack for work, hikes, parks, or a ski day. These no-bake oatmeal bars are easy to whip up and can be made in 30 minutes.

We really love this bar using sunflower seed butter for its taste, texture, and nutrients, but it's fun and delicious to use other butters, like peanut butter or cashew butter.

Line the bottom and sides of an 8-inch square baking pan with parchment paper and set aside.

In a large saucepan, melt the butter and sugar over medium heat. When the sugar has dissolved into the butter, add the vanilla and stir well. Add the oats, reduce heat to low, and cook for 5 minutes or until well combined and getting a bit sticky. Pour half of the oat mixture into the prepared pan and pat down evenly.

In a medium glass bowl, melt the chocolate chips and sunflower butter in the microwave: Start at 1 minute and stir, then continue to microwave in 30-second intervals, stirring in between each until completely melted and smooth.

Reserve about ¼ cup of the chocolate filling and pour the rest on top of the oat mixture in the pan. Spoon the remaining half of the oat mixture over the chocolate filling and spread around softly to even out. Drizzle the remaining chocolate on top. Refrigerate for a couple of hours to set. Store in an airtight container at room temperature for four days or in the fridge up to one week.

wish-I-were-in-the-florida-keys lime pie

ready in 2 hours, 30 minutes
serves 10

no-bake crust

1¾ cups graham
    cracker crumbs
6 tablespoons sugar
6 tablespoons unsalted
    butter, melted

filling

2 (8-ounce) blocks cream
    cheese, room temperature
½ cup Key lime juice (from
    about 20 Key limes)
1 (14-ounce) can sweetened
    condensed milk
1 teaspoon kosher salt
2 Key limes, for zesting
+ added yum:
    Whipped cream and
    Key lime slices

 **notes**

Sharon grew up in Florida and loves to share her love of Key lime pie! Few things taste like the Florida Keys more than this pie, and when you need warm sunshine, turquoise water, and a laid-back vibe, this pie will get you there. Truly authentic Key lime pie is a creamy pale yellow, so never trust a green Key lime pie! The only green should be flecks of Key lime zest.

make the crust

Combine the graham cracker crumbs, sugar, and melted butter in a bowl. Press the crumb mixture onto the bottom of a springform pan. No need to go up the sides; the two different layers look so beautiful.

make the filling

In a stand mixer or bowl with hand mixer, combine the cream cheese, lime juice, condensed milk, and salt. Mix well or until most of the cream cheese is smooth, but it's OK if there are still some small beads of cheese.

Scrape the cream cheese mixture onto the graham cracker crust. Zest the 2 limes on top of the pie. Refrigerate for at least 2 hours before serving. Store in an airtight container in the fridge up to three days.

+ added yum: Serve with a good dollop of whipped cream and garnish with Key lime slices.

tips

- Although this pie whips up quickly, juicing the Key limes can take some time since they don't have a lot of juice. Use a hand juicer if you have one. It's tedious (but worth it) to get juice out of Key limes.
- Use an electric mixer to ensure a creamy pie.
- For a gluten-free crust, just substitute crushed gluten-free graham crackers.

hey, wanna make a wine barrel herb garden?

Why start an herb garden? We believe fresh herbs add so much liveliness and flavor to just about any dish. Plus they're another way to add nutrition! People often skip buying fresh herbs because they are perishable, and some are pricey. We love everything about growing an herb garden big or small for those reasons.

If you don't have a lot of space, just grow a couple of different herbs in small pots. If you have a lot of space, consider growing herbs in your garden. We love a wine barrel herb garden because you can grow quite a few herbs without requiring too much maintenance or yard/patio space.

Here's how to make your own herb garden:

1. Get a wine barrel, preferably one already cut in half. (They are available at most Home Depots and Lowe's. If you live near a winery, see if they'll let you repurpose a used one for free.)

2. Turn the barrel so the opening is on the ground. Using a power drill, make about seven holes, spread out somewhat equally, for even drainage.

3. Spray the inside and outside of the barrel with apple cider vinegar (about 32 ounces) to discourage fungus growth.

4. Cover the inside bottom with a fabric or wire mesh so you don't lose a lot of your soil over time. Staple guns work great to secure the mesh.

5. Decide where it will go. Think of a spot with a lot of sunshine and plenty of drainage. It is especially important to be decisive before adding soil to the barrel; it gets very heavy once the soil is in there.

6. Lay a bed of rocks about 30 inches in diameter to lift the bottom of the barrel one to two inches from the ground to avoid it sitting directly in wet dirt; this helps prevent rot on the bottom of the barrel. If you're putting this on a deck, you may want to look online or in a hardware store for a barrel or large plant dolly with wheels/casters, or google how to add wheels/casters to the wine barrel. This will protect both your deck and the bottom of your wine barrel from rot.

7. Add fresh, organic potting soil. You'll need about four cubic feet. Make sure the soil is safe to grow food you'll be ingesting. You don't want to accidentally buy something with dangerous fertilizers.

8. Buy your favorite herbs (do a little research first to learn how they grow) and get those babies planted. The research will help you be strategic in their placement: tall ones in the back, the bossy ones over off to the side (i.e., oregano likes to take over), and the shorter trailing ones upfront so they don't get shaded.

9. You are now ready to be a proud, badass herb gardener and expert healthy home chef. Fresh herbs make great hostess gifts!

oregon wine country and its prestigious pinot noir

We are lucky enough to live right alongside Oregon's spectacular wine country and have enjoyed learning so much about Oregon's superstar grape, Pinot Noir.

Not only is Oregon Pinot Noir acclaimed, it's so versatile that it's a challenge to find a food that *doesn't* love being paired with it. If you get a chance, try enjoying some of our recipes with an Oregon Pinot Noir. You'll see why it unconventionally matches so beautifully with a large range of different foods.

> *Willamette Valley, Oregon's leading wine region, has two-thirds of the state's wineries and vineyards and is home to more than 700 wineries. It is recognized as one of the premier Pinot Noir-producing areas in the world. But why? Protected from cold Pacific Ocean air and rainstorms on the west by the Coast Range mountains, the Valley follows the Willamette River for more than a hundred miles from the Columbia River near Portland to just south of Eugene. The Cascade Range to the east forms a natural boundary and protects against the opposite extreme: the dry, desert-like climate of eastern Oregon. Overall, the climate boasts a long, gentle growing season: warm summers with cool evenings, a long and lovely autumn with the first rainfalls of winter amid plenty of sunny days, and mild winters followed by long springs. The unique geography and climate of this region led winegrowing pioneers like David Lett and Charles Coury to plant the first Pinot Noir grapes in the Willamette Valley more than 50 years ago.*

> —Willamette Valley Wineries Association

Should you ever find yourself planning a trip to Oregon, be sure the wine country is on your list of stops. The wines, landscape, vineyards, views, and tasting rooms are breathtaking. Reach out to us via email: (s.peddie@comcast.net) and we'll share our knowledge and help you develop an itinerary for a special day of wine tasting!

On the next page is a list of Willamette Valley Wineries we have visited and have personal experience with. To learn more about the 230+ Willamette Valley Wineries, check out willamettewines.com.

A fun day wine tasting in beautiful Oregon Wine Country

oregon winery tasting rooms we have visited:

Adelsheim Vineyard
Alexana
Alloro
Anne Amie Vineyards
Archery Summit
Argyle Winery
August Cellars
Beaux Frères
Belle Pente
Bella Vida
Bergstrom
Blakeslee
Brooks
De Ponte
Dobbes Family Estate
Domaine Divio
Domaine Drouhin
Domaine Roy & Fils
Domaine Serene
Duck Pond
Eola Hills

Erath
Eyrie Vineyards
Fairsing
Firesteed Cellars
Four Graces
Furioso
Gran Moraine
Hawks View
Hazel Fern
Hyland Estates
JK Carriere
Ken Wright
King Estate
Knudsen
Lachini
Lange
Lemelson Vineyards
Maragas
Oak Knoll
Oswego Hills
Penner-Ash

Ponzi
Raptor Ridge
Resonance
Rex Hill
Saffron Fields
Siduri
Sokol Blosser
Soléna
St. Innocent
Stoller
Sweet Cheeks
Torii Mor
Tresori
Trisaetum
Vista Hills
White Rose
WillaKenzie Estate
Willamette Valley Vineyard
Winderlea
Winters Hill

index

journaling pages

Cookbooks that have notes are like treasure chests and beautiful time capsules. We wanted to leave a couple of blank pages so you can record some special moments around food with your family and friends. Meals with loved ones make for the most special memories and stories. How fun if you can use a cookbook to share stories of Food, Family, and Friends with future generations, giving them a sense of who you were and where they came from!

acknowledgments

Never in a million years did we think we would have anything to thank covid-19 for, but here it goes. "Thank you, covid-19, for reminding us of what's truly important in life—Faith, Food, Family, and Friends. At first, there would have been another F word chosen for you, but these are where we landed. These are the words that got us through the pandemic and the words that prove to us that they will get us through everything. Because of you, our family is even closer, stronger, and more supportive of each other. We are more patient, resourceful, and creative. We are more independent, yet more open to real human connection. We are more healthful, helpful, and wise. We are more faithful, joyful, and compassionate. Most of all, we are more grateful ... for everything!"

Thank you to our extended family for all of the love and connections we feel even living across the country from all of you. We are a little team in Oregon but you always make us feel bigger and stronger. Thank you for always making us feel close from so far away. (An extra special thank you to Sharon's mom for always being her biggest cheerleader and making her feel she could do anything. That has been a great example to pass down in our family.)

A very special thank you to Aunt Dale and Cousin Barbara for helping us secure some of our family recipes and stories for this cookbook. Your love and interest were a warm hug and great support. Thank you for the Southern family love and all you have taught us over the years.

Thank you to all of our friends who inspire our cooking, traditions, and backyard fun. You have filled our years with purpose, important bonds, connection, love, support, and laughter.

Thank you to all of our friends and family who supported us on our cookbook journey. At times, this was an overwhelming process on top of our everyday lives and responsibilities. Each time you asked us about it, told us you believed in us, and just assumed it was going to happen, you encouraged us at the deepest level. Your support meant the world to us and kept us moving forward.

Thank you to all of the people and places that educated us. It has been amazing to see how each of those quilt pieces, stitched together, helped us make a beautiful project to be proud of. *Go Gators! Go Ducks! Go Frogs!*

Thank you to Deri, Heather, Julie, and Dorothy. Each of you touched our cookbook with your expertise, dedication, and talents. You helped us bring our cookbook to the professional level we dreamed of. Thank you for believing in us. Thank you for humbly and graciously guiding us. This is girl power at its most admirable level.

Thank you to our dear, very fun, and very talented friend Suzanne Young of Suzanne Young Photography for taking our cover photo and headshots for our book and marketing. And, you did it in the middle of moving! xoxo

Thank you to Tom, the best, most devoted, most loving, most supportive hubby and dad a family could ever wish for. Thank you for being our number one taste tester and hype man! Thank you for scouring shelves during covid-19 for just the right ingredients we needed. For two years, you patiently waited to eat while we got the right staging, lighting, and shot. Thank you for believing in us and supporting us every step of the way.

Thank you to one of our other favorite F words, our loving and loyal pup, Finley. You came into our lives with perfect timing, healing our hearts after we lost Maggie. We could have never made it through a pandemic without the special love and comfort of a dog like you. You are the perfect example of why *Dog* is *God* spelled backward.

Last, but most important, thank you, God, for our family. Thank you for giving us to each other. Thank you for the love and closeness we share. Thank you for our home. Thank you for this special experience together. Thank you for our cookbook. Thank you, God, for our food, family, and friends.

about the authors

Sharon Caldwell Peddie is the author of *Grow Yourself Beautiful: A Smart Girl's Guide to Following Her Heart and Focusing on Her Inner Joy.* She wrote the book as a passionate advocate for young women and the challenges they face in today's world. The book was a Pacific Book Review finalist, receiving first runner-up for Best Nonfiction, and has received exceptional professional reviews. Sharon has also written inspirational articles for lifestyle magazines.

In addition to dedicating 30 years to raising her three daughters, Sharon has spent 20+ years working closely with girls ages five to 18 in many capacities. Her growing brand and platform as an author are helping to inspire people of all ages to continually grow themselves and their lives in ways that feel meaningfully beautiful to them.

Sharon earned a journalism and public relations degree from the University of Florida. In addition to writing, she is a lifelong foodie with a passion for cooking. She believes cooking builds self-love, self-confidence, self-esteem, good health, and strong connections, which is why it was important to her for all three of her daughters to be strong cooks in their development to becoming strong women.

Sharon is an avid gardener and an enthusiastic entertainer who loves to create beautiful dinner parties in her backyard garden. She attributes her knowledge and confidence in entertaining to the experience she's gained by just doing it a lot and to being an event planner for nonprofit organizations for over 25 years. She grew up in Florida and lives in Oregon.

Kelsey Peddie is a practicing attorney at a firm in Portland, Oregon, specializing in business and employment litigation. She graduated from the University of Oregon with a journalism degree and received her law degree from Lewis & Clark Law School. In her free time, Kelsey is also a judge and mentor for the Jessup Competition, an international moot court that gathers teams from over 100 countries. Kelsey is a dedicated foodie and cook who enjoys learning from fellow foodies and chefs through Instagram, cookbooks, and the Food Network. Kelsey loves working on the renovation of her home, cooking for friends, and is a passionate gardener, growing her own vegetables, herbs, and flowers.

Kendall Peddie graduated with a degree in coordinated dietetics from Texas Christian University, where she also completed her dietetic internship. She is a registered dietitian working as a nutrition consultant in corporate wellness. Kendall is also currently studying to earn her master's degree in applied physiology and kinesiology from the University of Florida. Her studies and work experience allow her to keep up with and vet the latest, most credible food and nutrition-related information. Her professional website (wellfeddie.com) and Instagram account (@well.feddie.rdn) provide personal inspiration, professional dietetic information, and recipes for food, mind, body, and soul. She's extremely passionate about food, nutrition, and caring for others on their journey and relationship with food.

Cameron Peddie is studying strategic communications with a minor in studio art at Texas Christian University. She is a talented, creative artist who is interested in helping companies develop their visual brand identity. Cameron is foodie #4 and especially enjoys the artistic side of creating beautiful dishes with gorgeous colors and textures. Her first experiences in the kitchen were baking; it is still one of her strategies to reduce stress and share joy and goodies with her friends. Cami loves creating art to inspire joy and positivity.

let's stay in touch

websites

sharoncaldwellpeddie.com

sharonpeddieblog.com

Wellfeddie.com

instagram

@author_sharoncaldwellpeddie

@well.feddie.rdn

@camipeddieart

pinterest

Author Sharon Caldwell Peddie

Kelsey Peddie

Well Feddie Kendall Peddie, RDN

Cami Peddie

facebook

Author Sharon Caldwell Peddie

twitter

@SCPeddie

hashtags

#fwordsmomletussay

#growyourselfbeautiful

#growyourlifebeautiful